# TRISTAN UND ISOLDE
## Vocal Score

RICHARD WAGNER

Includes the only translation of the singing text authorized
by Wagner's heirs for performance in the English language

DOVER PUBLICATIONS, INC.
Mineola, New York

*Bibliographical Note*

This Dover edition, first published in 2003, reprints all the music of *Tristan and Isolda by Richard Wagner / Vocal Score by R. Kleinmichel / English—German / English translation by H. and F. Corder*, originally published by Breitkopf & Härtel, Leipzig, n.d. The title page of this publication includes the following note: "The present translation of 'Tristan and Isolda' is the only authorised one by Richard Wagner's heirs as lawful owners of the copyrights for the representations and performances in English language." Lists of credits, characters, and contents—all newly added—are based on information given in *The New Grove Book of Operas,* edited by Stanley Sadie, copyright © 1992, 1996, 2000 by Macmillan Press Ltd., and published by St. Martin's Press, New York. We are indebted to Amherst College, Amherst, Mass. and Brown University Music Library, Providence, R.I., for providing us with this rare edition for republication.

*International Standard Book Number: 0-486-42664-5*

Manufactured in the United States of America
Dover Publications, Inc., 31 East 2nd Street, Mineola, N.Y. 11501

# TRISTAN UND ISOLDE

*Handlung (drama)* in three acts

Music by

## RICHARD WAGNER

*Tristan's* libretto is by the composer, based on ancient legend, probably of Celtic origin, in the version by Gottfried von Strassburg (13th c.). The prose scenario was begun on 20 August 1857 and the poem completed on 18 September. Each of the drama's three acts was completed and engraved, in sequence, before the next act was sketched. The full score of Act 1 was completed on 3 April 1858 in Zurich; of Act 2 on 18 March 1859, in Venice; and of Act 3 on 6 August 1859 in Lucerne. Fritz Mottl conducted the first performance at Bayreuth in 1886.

### CHARACTERS

| | |
|---|---|
| Isolde, *daughter of the Queen of Ireland, brought to Cornwall to marry King Mark* | Soprano |
| Brangäne, *Isolde's maid and confidante* | Soprano |
| Tristan, *a knight, nephew of King Mark, sent to accompany Isolde* | Tenor |
| Melot, *a knight, the King's courier* | Tenor |
| Kurvenal, *Tristan's faithful squire* | Baritone |
| King Mark, *King of Cornwall* | Bass |
| A Young Sailor | Tenor |
| A Shepherd | Tenor |
| A Steersman | Baritone |

Sailors, knights, squires, people of the court.

*Setting: At sea, and in Cornwall and Brittany during the Middle Ages*

## SETTINGS OF THE ACTS
*Scenes and Characters*

### FIRST ACT
### 1

*At sea, on the deck of Tristan's ship,*
*during the crossing from Ireland to Cornwall*



### SECOND ACT
### 94

*King Mark's royal castle in Cornwall*



### THIRD ACT
### 197

*Tristan's castle in Brittany*



**END OF DRAMA**

# TRISTAN UND ISOLDE
Vocal Score

# Tristan and Isolda. | Tristan und Isolde.

Drama in three Acts | Handlung in drei Aufzügen

by | von

## RICHARD WAGNER.

English translation by H. & F. Corder.

## First Act._ Erster Aufzug.

### Introduction. | Einleitung.

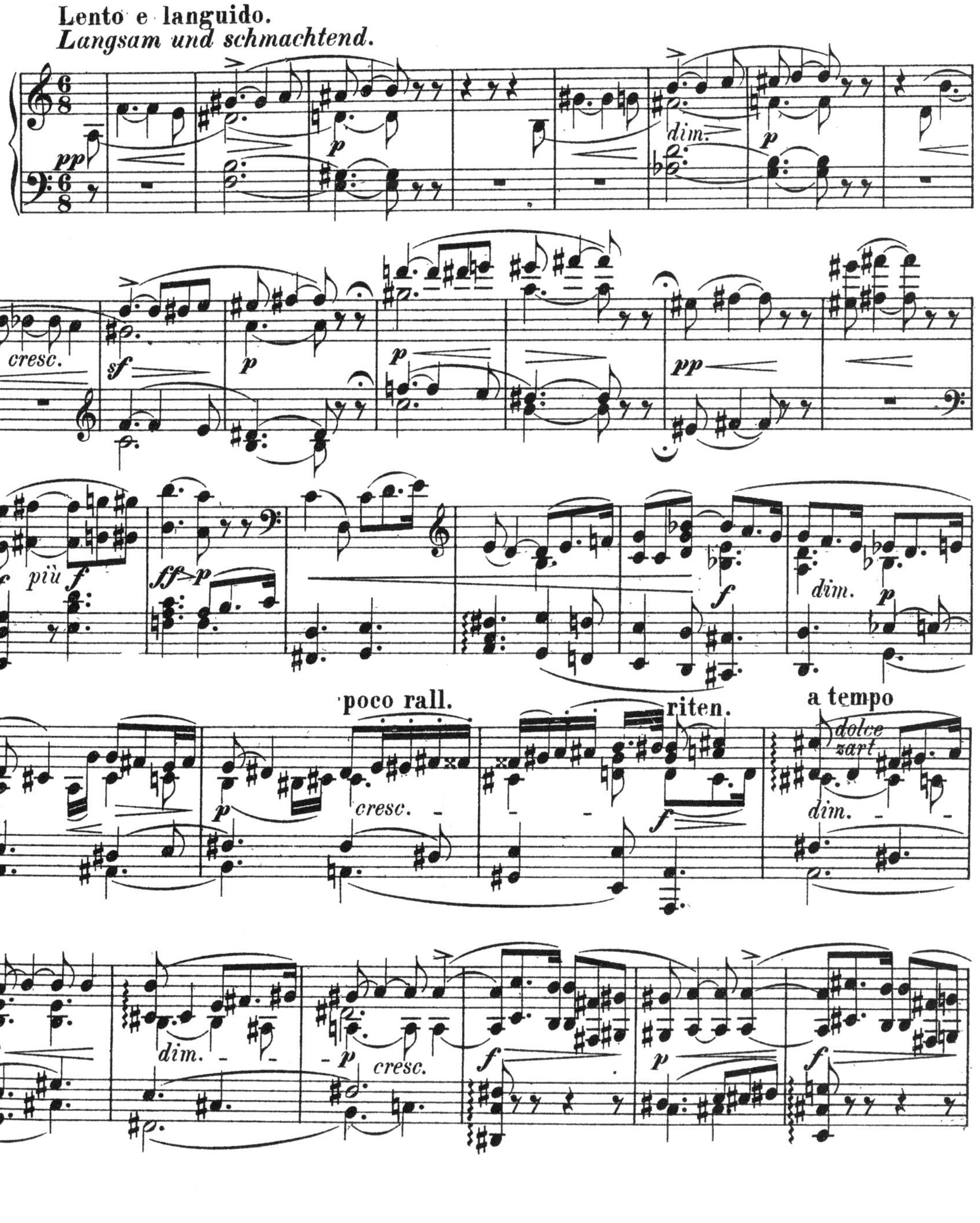

**Lento e languido.**
*Langsam und schmachtend.*

poco rall.

riten.

a tempo

*dolce zart*

espress.
cresc.
dolce
zart
ten.
dim.
animato
belebt
Animando.
Belebend,
cresc.
molto cresc.
rallent.
a tempo
dolce
zart
dim.
dim.
cresc.
cresc.
meno f
espress.
sempre più f
più f

marcato
f
f
più f
più f
molto espress.
ff
sempre f
più f

più f

ff

espress.

**Il tempo poco a poco ritenuto.**
***Allmählich im Zeitmass etwas zurückhaltend.***

dim.

trem.

dolce
zart

p

cresc.

dim.

f

più p

pp

(The Curtain rises.)
*(Der Vorhang geht auf.)*

# Scene I. | Erste Scene.

(A pavilion erected on the deck of a ship richly hung with tapestry, quite closed in at back at first. A narrow hatchway at one side leads below into the cabin.
Isolda on a couch, her face buried in the cushions. — Brangæna, holding open a curtain, looks over the side of the vessel.)

*(Zeltartiges Gemach auf dem Vorderdeck eines Seeschiffes, reich mit Teppichen behangen, beim Beginn nach dem Hintergrunde zu gänzlich geschlossen; zur Seite führt eine schmale Treppe in den Schiffsraum hinab.
Isolde auf einem Ruhebett, das Gesicht in die Kissen gedrückt. — Brangäne, einen Teppich zurückgeschlagen haltend, blickt zur Seite über den Bord.)*

**Andante moderato.**
***Mässig langsam.***

THE VOICE OF A YOUNG SAILOR (from above, as if from the mast-head).
*STIMME EINES JUNGEN SEEMANNS (aus der Höhe, wie vom Maste her vernehmbar).*

Tenor.
(energico)
(kräftig)
Westward sur - ges slip, eastward speeds the ship. The wind so wild blows
Westwärts schweift der Blick, ostwärts streicht das Schiff. Frisch weht der Wind der
(calando)
(nachlassend)
(poco steso)
(etwas gedehnt)
homeward now:— my I-rish child, where wait-est thou? Say, must our sails be weighted,
Hei-math zu:— mein i-risch Kind, wo wei-lest du? Sind's dei-ner Seuf-zer We-hen,
fill'd by thy sighs un - bat-ed?— Waft us, wind strong and wild!— Woe, ah
die mir die Se-gel blä-hen?— We-he, we-he, du Wind!— Weh, ach
(con fuoco)
(feurig)
woe for my child!— O I-rish maid!— my winsome, mar-vellous
we-he, mein Kind!— I-ri-sche Maid,— du wil-de, min-ni-ge
Vivace.
Lebhaft.
ISOLDA (starting up suddenly).
ISOLDE (jäh auffahrend).
(She looks round in agitation.)
(Sie blickt verstört um sich.)
maid! What wight dares in - sult me?
Maid! Wer wagt mich zu höhnen?
dim.
Moderato.
Mässig.
Brangæ-na, ho!— Say, where sail we?
Brangä-ne, du?— Sag, wo sind wir?

BRANGÆNA (at the opening).
BRANGÄNE (an der Öffnung).
Bluish stripes are stretch - ing a - long the west; swift - ly the ship sails to the shore; if rest - ful the sea by eve we shall read - i - ly set foot on land. Cornwall's ver - dant strand.
Blaue Strei - fen stie - gen im We - sten auf; sanft und schnell se - gelt das Schiff; auf ru - hi - ger See vor A - bend er - rei - chen wir si - cher das Land. Kornwalls grü - nen Strand.
ISOLDA.
ISOLDE.
What land?
Welches Land?
Presto.
Schnell.
Nev - er more! To-day nor
Nim - mermehr! Nicht heut', noch
p
f

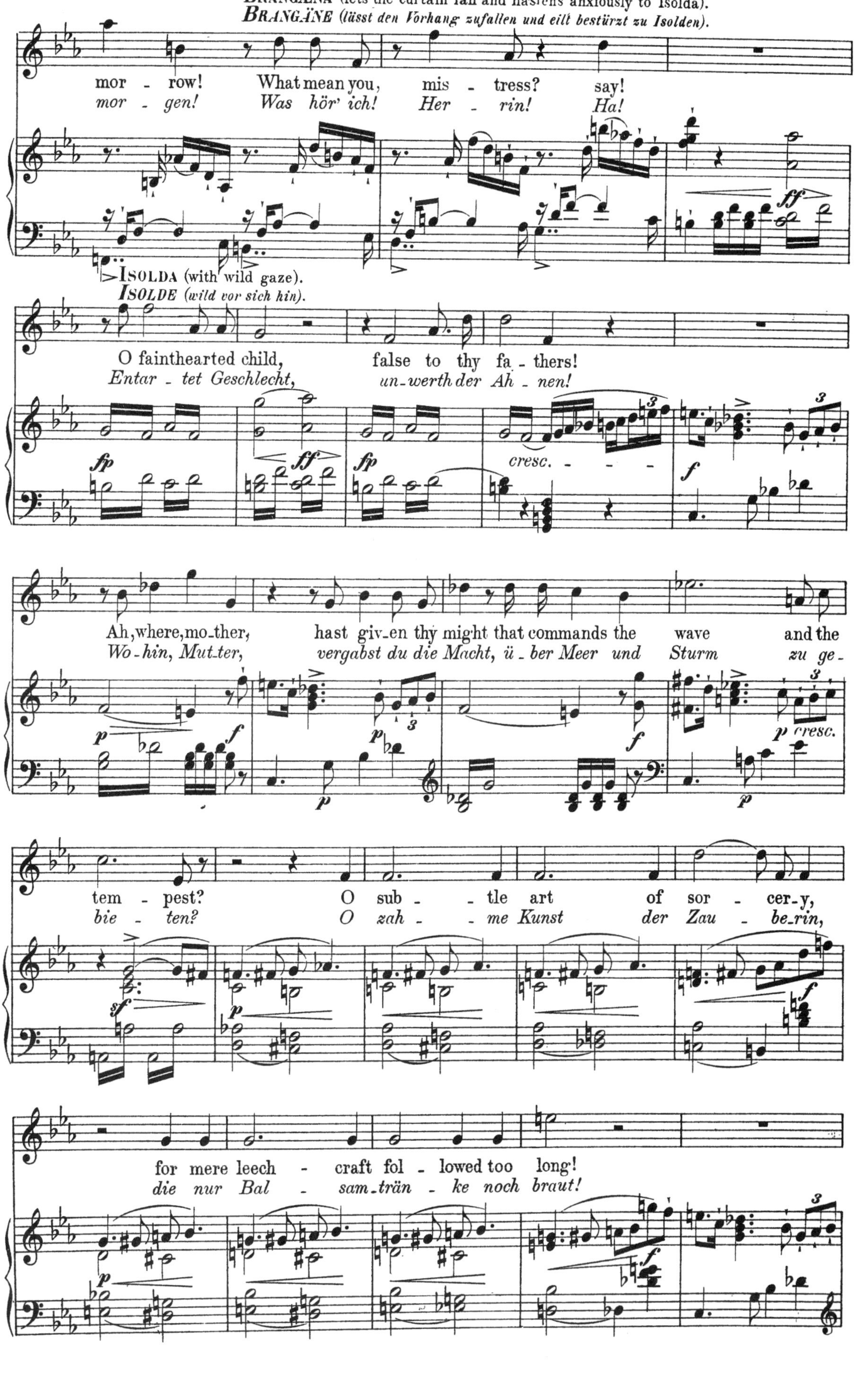

BRANGÆNA (lets the curtain fall and hastens anxiously to Isolda).
BRANGÄNE (lässt den Vorhang zufallen und eilt bestürzt zu Isolden).
morrow! What mean you, mistress? say!
morgen! Was hör' ich! Herrin! Ha!
ff
ISOLDA (with wild gaze).
ISOLDE (wild vor sich hin).
O fainthearted child, false to thy fathers!
Entartet Geschlecht, unwerth der Ahnen!
fp
ff
fp
cresc.
f
Ah, where, mother, hast given thy might that commands the wave and the
Wohin, Mutter, vergabst du die Macht, über Meer und Sturm zu ge-
p
f
p
f
p cresc.
p
tempest? O subtle art of sorcery,
bieten? O zahme Kunst der Zauberin,
sf
p
f
for mere leechcraft followed too long!
die nur Balsamtränke noch braut!
p
f

Awake in me once more, pow - er of will! a - rise
Erwa - che mir wie - der, küh - ne Ge - walt; herauf
cresc.
from thy hid - - - ing within my breast!
aus dem Bu - - - sen, wo du dich bargst!
più f
Hark to my bid - - ding, flut - - tering
Hört mei - nen Wil - - len, za - - gende
ff
bree - zes! A - rise and storm in boi - sterous
Win - de! Her - an zu Kampf und Wet - - ter-ge-
strife! With fu - ri-ous rage and hur - ricane's hur-tle
tös', zu to - ben-der Stür - me wü - thendem Wirbel!

wa - ken the sea from slum - ber-ing calm, rouse up the deep to its
Treibt aus dem Schlaf dies träu - men-de Meer, weckt aus dem Grund sei-ne
p
f
p
f
p cresc.
dev - il-ish deeds! Shew it the prey which glad - ly I prof - fer!
grol - len-de Gier! Zeigt ihm die Beu - te, die ich ihm bie - te!
più f
Be shat ter'd this arrogant ship and en-
Zer-schlag' es dies trot-zi-ge Schiff, des zer-
ff
f
shrined in o - cean each shred!
schell - ten Trüm-mer verschling's!
ff
And woe to the lives! their wavering death-sighs I leave to ye winds as your
Und was auf ihm lebt, den wehenden A-them, den lass' ich euch Win - den zum
dim.
p
f
f

BRANGÆNA (in extreme alarm and concern for Isolda).
BRANGÄNE (im äussersten Schreck um Isolden sich bemühend).
lot! Alas! Ah! Ah, I've ever dreaded some
Lohn! O weh! Ach! Ach des Übels, das ich ge-
ff
ff
dim.
ill! Isolda! Mistress! Heart of mine! What
ahnt! Isolde! Herrin! Theures Herz! Was
p
cresc.
Poco a poco più moderato.
Allmählich etwas mässiger im Zeitmass.
secret dost thou hide? Without a tear thou'st quitted thy father and mother, and scarce a
bargst du mir so lang? Nicht eine Thräne weintest du Vater und Mutter; kaum einen
f
f
dim.
p
mf
word of farewell to friends thou gav'st; leaving home thou
Gruss den Bleibenden botest du: von der Heimath
f
dim.
p
p
sf
sf
sf
stood'st how cold and still! pale and speechless
scheidend kalt und stumm, bleich und schweigend
sf
sf
sf
sf

on the way,
auf der Fahrt,
food re - ject - ing,
oh - ne Nah - rung,
sf
cresc.
Animando.
Belebend.
reft of sleep,
oh - ne Schlaf,
stern and wretch - ed,
starr und e - lend,
wild, dis - turbed:
wild ver - stört:
how it
wie er -
dim.
Più moderato.
Müssiger.
pains me so to see thee!
trug ich, so dich se - hend,
friends no more we seem,
nichts dir mehr zu sein,
p
f
be - ing thus e - stranged.
fremd vor dir zu steh'n?
Make me part - ner in thy
O, nun mel - de, was dich
mf
dim.

p
pain! Tell me freely all thy fears! Lady, thou hear-est, sweet-est and
müht! Sa-ge, künde, was dich quält! Herrin I-sol-de, trau-te-ste
p
cresc.
ff
dim.
dear-est! If for true friend you take me, your con-fidant O
Hol-de, soll sie werth sich dir wähnen, ver-trau-e nun Bran-
dim.
p
dolce
p
Animando con impeto.
Heftig belebend.
ISOLDA.
ISOLDE.
make me! Air! air! or my heart will
gä-nen! Luft! Luft! Mir er-stickt das
sf
sf
p
cresc.
choke! O-pen! o-pen there wide!
Herz! Öff-ne! Öff-ne dort weit!
(Brangaena hastily
(Brangäne zieht ei-
ff
draws the curtains in the centre apart.)
lig die Vorhänge in der Mitte auseinander.)
dim.
p

# Scene II. | Zweite Scene.

(The whole length of the ship is now seen, down to the stern, with the sea and horizon beyond. Round the mainmast in the middle are seamen, busied with ropes; beyond them in the stern are seen knights and attendants seated, like the sailors; a little apart Tristan stands with folded arms and thoughtfully gazing out to sea; at his feet Kurvenal reclines carelessly. From the mast-head above is heard once more the voice of the young sailor.)

*(Man blickt dem Schiff entlang bis zum Steuerbord, über den Bord hinaus auf das Meer und den Horizont. Um den Hauptmast in der Mitte ist Seevolk, mit Tauen beschäftigt, gelagert: über sie hinaus gewahrt man am Steuerbord Ritter und Knappen, ebenfalls gelagert, von ihnen etwas entfernt Tristan, mit verschränkten Armen stehend, und sinnend in das Meer blickend, zu Füssen ihm, nachlässig gelagert, Kurwenal. Vom Maste her, aus der Höhe, vernimmt man wieder die Stimme des jungen Seemannes.)*

now re - mov - ed, — brave and bright, — cow - ard knight! —
mir ver - lo - ren, — hehr und heil, — kühn und feig! —
p
poco cresc.
cresc.
(laughing unnaturally)
(unheimlich lachend)
f
p
Death - de - vot - ed head! — Death - de - vot - ed heart! — Think'st high - ly of yon
Tod — ge - weihtes Haupt! — Tod — ge - weihtes Herz! — Was hältst du von dem
ff
p
p
pp
Isolda.
Isolde.
minion? There, that he - ro, who from mine eyes a - verts his
Knechte? Dort den Hel - den, der mei - nem Blick den sei - nen
Brangæna (following her glance).
Brangäne (ihrem Blicke folgend).
Whom mean'st thou?
Wen meinst du?
p espress.
pp
own: in shrink - ing shame my gaze he shuns. — Say, how
birgt, in Scham und Scheu - e ab - wärts schaut. — Sag', wie

BRANGÆNA.
BRANGÄNE.
hold you him? Mean you Sir Tristan, lady mine? Extoll'd by ev'ry
dünkt er dich? Frägst du nach Tristan, theu-re Frau? dem Wun-der al-ler
p cresc.
mf
nation, his happy country's pride, the hero of creation, whose
Rei-che, dem hoch-ge-pries'nen Mann, dem Helden oh-ne Gleiche, des
sf
p
sf
ISOLDA (mocking her).
ISOLDE (sie verhöhnend).
In shrinking trepidation his shame he seeks to
Der zagend vor dem Streiche sich flüchtet wo er
fame so high and wide?
Ruh-mes Hort und Bann?
p
sfp
p
hide, while to the king, his relation, he brings the corpse-like
kann, weil ei-ne Braut er als Lei-che für sei-nen Herrn ge-
cresc.
f
sf

bride!— Seems it so senseless what I-say? Go ask him-
wann! Dünkt es dich dun-kel, mein Ge-dicht? Frag' ihn denn
ff dim.
p
self, our gracious host, dare he ap-proach my side? No courteous heed or loy-al
selbst, den frei-en Mann, ob mir zu nah'n er wagt? Der Eh-ren Gruss und zücht'ge
f
p
f
(poco steso)
(etwas gedehnt)
care this he-ro t'wards his la-dy turns; but to meet her his heart is
Acht ver-gisst der Her-rin der za-ge Held, dass ihr Blick ihn nur nicht er-
cresc.
p
daunted, this knight so high-ly vaunted!— Oh,— he wots well the
rei-che, den Hel-den oh-ne Glei-che!— O,— er weiss wohl, war-
ff
p
più p
pp
cause!— To the trai-tor go, bearing his la-dy's will! As my ser-vant
um!— Zu dem Stol-zen geh', meld' ihm der Her-rin Wort! Mei-nem Dienst be-
p

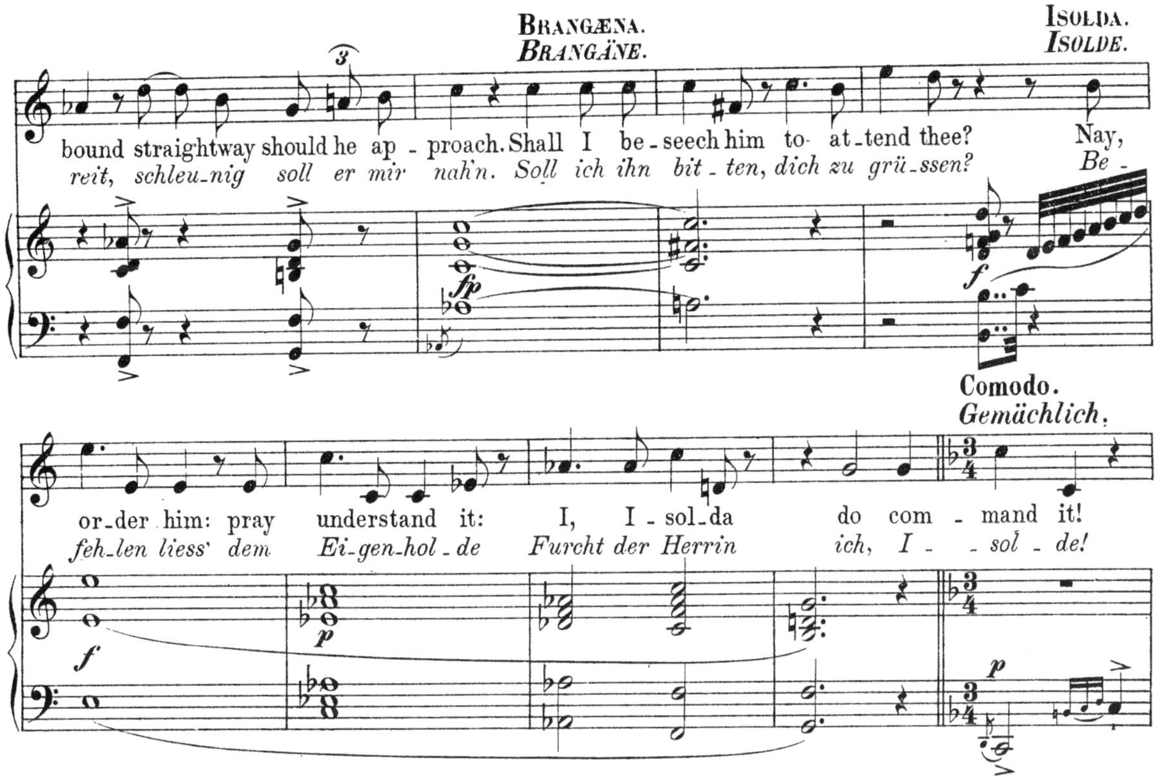

BRANGÆNA.
BRANGÄNE.
ISOLDA.
ISOLDE.
bound straightway should he ap - proach. Shall I be - seech him to - at - tend thee? Nay,
reit, schleu - nig soll er mir nah'n. Soll ich ihn bit - ten, dich zu grü - ssen? Be -
Comodo.
Gemächlich.
or - der him: pray understand it: I, I - sol - da do com - mand it!
feh - len liess' dem Ei - gen - hol - de Furcht der Herrin ich, I - - sol - de!

(At an imperious sign from Isolda Brangæna withdraws and timidly walks along the deck towards the stern, past the working sailors. Isolda, following her with fixed gaze, sinks back on the couch, where she remains sitting during the following, her eyes still turned sternward.)
*(Auf Isolde's gebieterischen Wink entfernt sich Brangäne und schreitet verschämt den Deck entlang dem Steuerbord zu, an den arbeitenden Seeleuten vorbei. Isolde, mit starrem Blicke ihr folgend, zieht sich rücklings nach dem Ruhebett zurück, wo sie sitzend während des Folgenden bleibt, das Auge unabgewandt nach dem Steuerbord gerichtet.)*

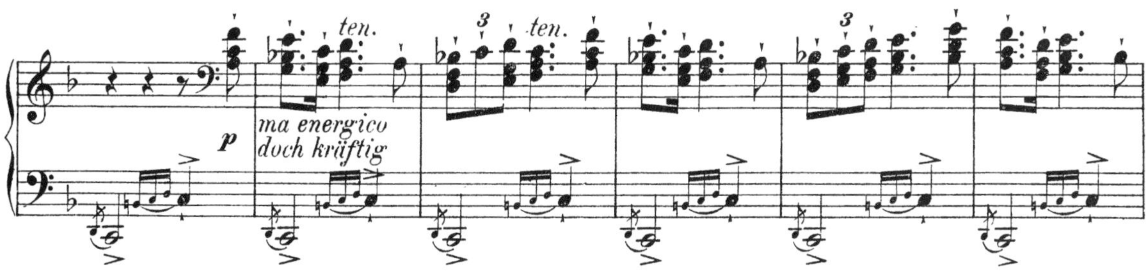


(Kurvenal, observing Brangæna's approach, plucks Tristan by the robe without rising.)
*(Kurwenal, der Brangänen kommen sieht, zupft, ohne sich zu erheben, Tristan am Gewande.)*

KURVENAL.
KURWENAL.
Be-ware, Tris - - - tan! Message from I-sol - da!
Hab' Acht, Tri - - - stan! Botschaft von I-sol - de.
cresc.
sf
TRISTAN (starting).
TRISTAN (auffahrend).
What is't? I - sol - da?
Was ist? I - sol - de?
(He quickly composes himself as Brangaena approaches and curtsies to him.)
(Er fasst sich schnell, als Brangäne vor ihm anlangt und sich verneigt.)
rallent.
p
Andante moderato.
Mässig langsam.
What would my la - dy? I, her liegeman, fain will listen
Von mei-ner Her-rin? Ihr ge-hor-sam was zu hö-ren
f
p
while her loy - al woman tells her will.
mel-det hö - fisch mir die trau - te Magd?
BRANGÆNA.
BRANGÄNE.
My lord, Sir
Mein Her - re
Tris-tan, Dame I - sol - da would have speech with you at
Tri-stan, euch zu se - hen wünscht I - - sol - de, mei - ne

TRISTAN.
TRISTAN.
Is she with travel worn? The end is near: nay, ere the set of
Grämt sie die lange Fahrt, die geht zu End; eh noch die Son-ne
once.
Frau.
p
sun, sight we the land. All that your mistress commands me, trust me, I shall
sinkt, sind wir am Land. Was mei-ne Frau mir be-feh-le, treu-lich sei's er-
p
p
BRANGÆNA.
BRANGÄNE.
That you, Sir Tristan, go to her, this is my la-dy's wish.
So mög' Herr Tristan zu ihr geh'n: das ist der Her-rin Will'.
TRISTAN.
TRISTAN.
mind.
füllt.
Where yon-der
Wo dort die
p
verdant meadows in dis-tance dim are mounting, waits my sovreign
grünen Flu-ren dem Blick noch blau sich fär-ben, harrt mein Kö-nig
mf
p
mf

for his mate: to lead her to his presence I'll wait up - on the princess;
meiner Frau: zu ihm sie zu ge - lei - ten, bald nah' ich mich der Lich - ten;
dim.
p
BRANGÆNA.
BRANGÄNE.
My lord, Sir Tristan, list to me: this one
Mein Her - re Tristan, hö - re wohl: dei - ne
'tis an hon - our all my own.
Kei - nem gönnt' ich die - se Gunst.
p
cresc.
thing my la - dy wills, that thou at once attend her, there where she waits for thee.
Dien - ste will die Frau, dass du zur Stell' ihr nahtest, dort, wo sie dei - ner harrt.
TRISTAN.
TRISTAN.
In a - ny
Auf je - der
f
f
f
f
p
sf
station where I stand I tru - ly serve but her, the pearl of woman -
Stel - le, wo ich steh', ge - treu - lich dien' ich ihr, der Frau - en höchster
sf espress.
dim.
p dolce

hood. If I un - heeding left the helm how might I
Ehr! Liess ich das Steu_er jetzt zur Stund, wie lenkt' ich
sf
f
sf
sf
sf
sf
dim.
BRANGÆNA.
BRANGÄNE.
pi_lot her ship in surety to King Mark? Tris - tan, my mas - ter;
si_cher den Kiel zu Kö_nig Marke's Land? Tri - stan, mein Her - re,
p
f
accel.
why mock - est me? Seem_eth my saying obscure to you, list to my
was höhnst du mich? Dünkt dich nicht deutlich die thör'ge Magd, hör' meiner
trem.
f
p
accel.
sf
p
sf
p
cresc.
la - dy's words! Thus, look you, she hath spoken: "Go
Her - rin Wort! So, hiess sie, sollt' ich sa_gen: Be -
f
f
f
f
Steso.
Gedehnt.
or - der him, and understand it, I, I - sol - da, do com -
feh - len liess' dem Ei_genhol - de Furcht der Her_rin sie, I -
f
p

Vivace, ma non troppo presto.
Lebhaft, doch nicht zu schnell.
TRISTAN (tranquillo).
TRISTAN (ruhig).
mand it?"
sol - de.
What wouldst thou wish to re - ply?
Was wohl er - wi - der- test du?
KURVENAL (sprining up).
KURWENAL (aufspringend).
May I an answer make her?
Darf ich die Antwort sa - gen?
KURVENAL.
KURWENAL.
Thus should she say to Dame I sold':
Das sa - ge sie der Frau I - sold':
Though Cornwall's crown and
Wer Kornwalls Kron' und
Eng - land's isle for Ireland's child he chose, his own by choice she
Eng - lands Erb' an Ir-lands Maid ver - macht, der kann der Magd nicht
may not be: he brings the King his bride. A he - ro - knight
ei - gen sein, die selbst dem Ohm er schenkt. Ein Herr der Welt

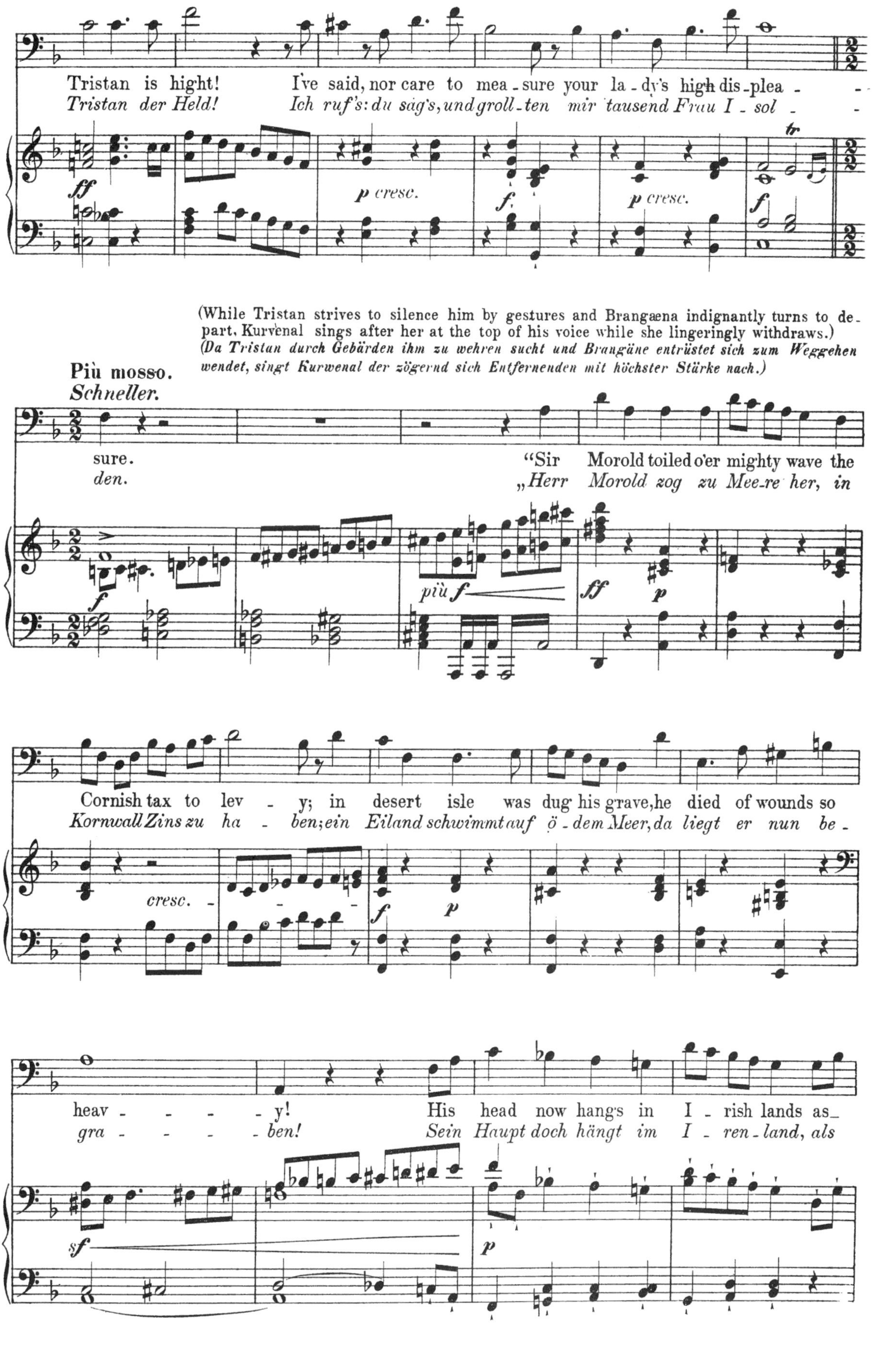

Tristan is hight! I've said, nor care to mea - sure your la - dy's high dis - plea -
*Tristan der Held! Ich ruf's: du säg's, und groll - ten mir tausend Frau I - sol -*

*ff* *p cresc.* *f* *p cresc.* *f* *tr*

(While Tristan strives to silence him by gestures and Brangaena indignantly turns to depart, Kurvenal sings after her at the top of his voice while she lingeringly withdraws.)
*(Da Tristan durch Gebärden ihm zu wehren sucht und Brangäne entrüstet sich zum Weggehen wendet, singt Kurwenal der zögernd sich Entfernenden mit höchster Stärke nach.)*

**Più mosso.**
*Schneller.*

sure. "Sir Morold toiled o'er mighty wave the
*den. „Herr Morold zog zu Mee - re her, in*

*f* *più f* *ff* *p*

Cornish tax to lev - y; in desert isle was dug his grave, he died of wounds so
Kornwall Zins zu ha - ben; ein Eiland schwimmt auf ö - dem Meer, da liegt er nun be -
cresc.
f
p

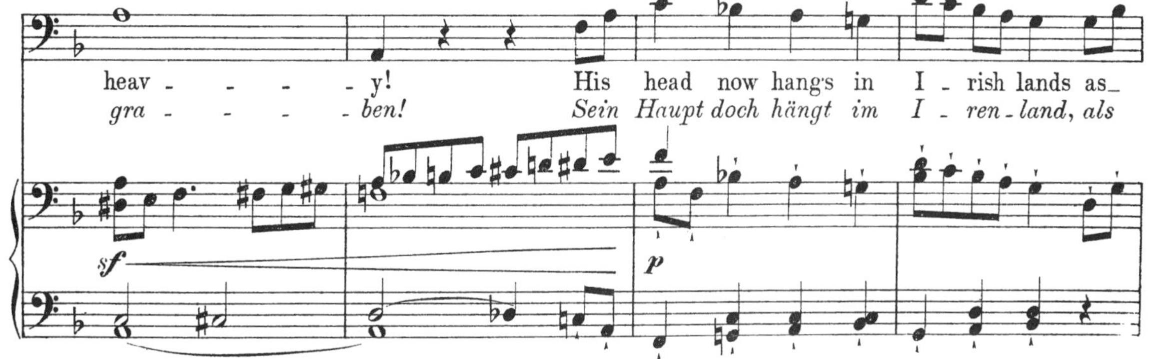
heav - - - - y! His head now hangs in I - rish lands as
gra - - - - ben! Sein Haupt doch hängt im I - ren - land, als
sf
p

wereg'ild won at English hands. Bravo, our brave Tristan! Let his tax take who
Zins gezahlt von En-ge-land. Heil unser Held Tristan, wie der Zins zah-len
cresc.
ff

(Kurvenal, scolded away by Tristan, descends into the cabin; Brangæna returns in agitation to Isolda, closing the curtains behind her while the whole crew without is heard singing.)
*(Kurwenal, von Tristan fortgescholten, ist in den Schiffsraum hinabgestiegen: Brangäne, in Bestürzung zu Isolde zurückgekehrt, schliesst hinter sich die Vorhänge, während die ganze Mannschaft aussen sich hören lässt.)*

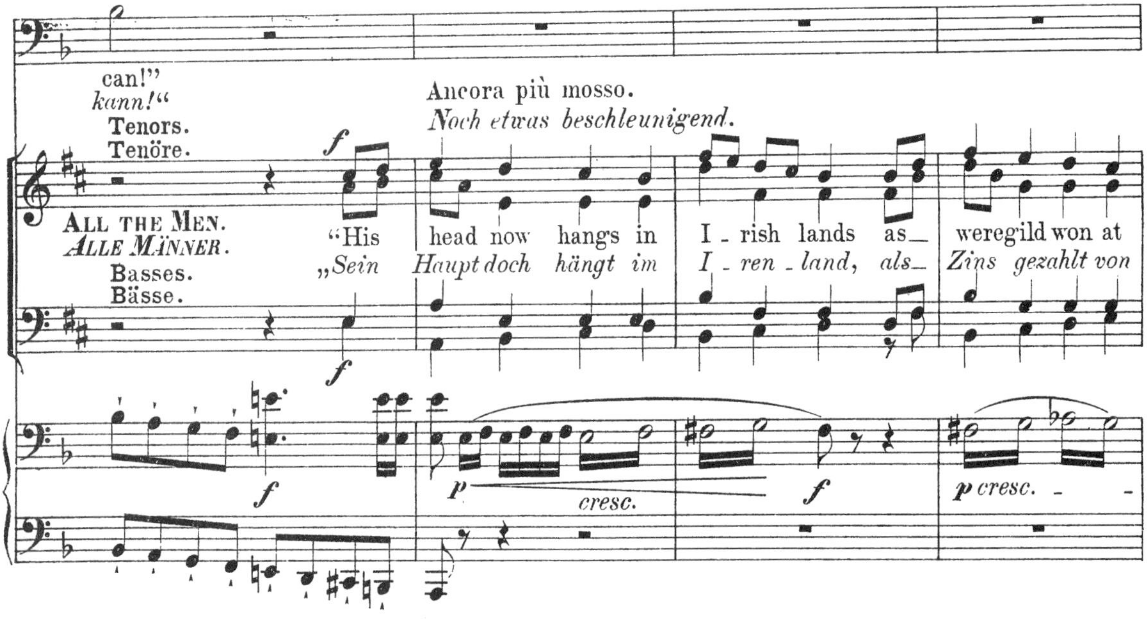

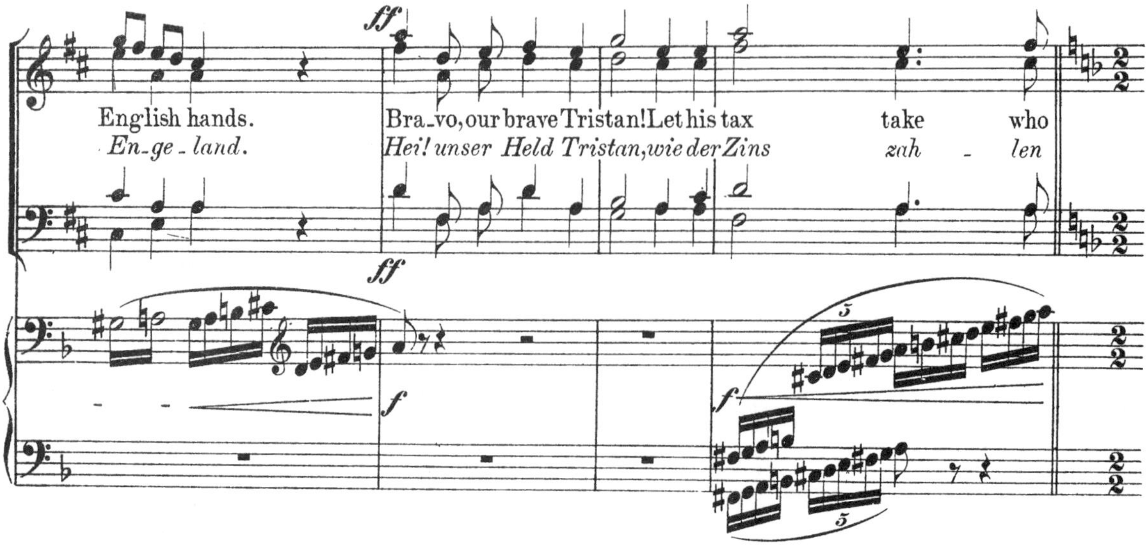

can!"
*kann!"*

Ancora più mosso.
*Noch etwas beschleunigend.*

Tenors.
Tenöre.

ALL THE MEN.
*ALLE MÄNNER.*

Basses.
Bässe.

f

"His head now hangs in I-rish lands as weregild won at
*„Sein Haupt doch hängt im I-ren-land, als Zins gezahlt von*

f

f p cresc. f p cresc.

ff

English hands. Bra-vo, our brave Tristan! Let his tax take who
*En-ge-land. Hei! unser Held Tristan, wie der Zins zah-len*

ff

f

Allegro molto.
*Sehr lebhaft.*

# Scene III. | Dritte Scene.

can!"
*kann!"*
(Isolda and Brangæna alone, with the curtains completely closed.)
(Isolda rises with a despairing gesture of wrath. Brangæna falls at her feet.)
*(Isolde und Brangäne allein, bei vollkommen wieder geschlossenen Vorhängen.)*
*(Isolde erhebt sich mit verzweiflungsvoller Wuthgebärde. Brangäne stürzt ihr zu Füssen.)*
ff
ff
ff
BRANGÆNA.
*BRANGÄNE.*
Ah! an answer so in-
*Weh! ach we-he! dies zu*
ff
dim.
sult - - ing!
*dul - - den!*
p
cresc.
ISOLDA (checking herself on the point of a fearful outburst).
*ISOLDE (dem furchtbarsten Ausbruch nahe, schnell sich zusammenraffend).*
più f
BRANGÆNA.
*BRANGÄNE.*
And now, of Tristan! I'd know if he de-nies me. Ah, ques-tion not!
*Doch nun von Tristan! Ge-nau will ich's ver-neh-men. Ach, fra-ge nicht!*
ff
dim.
p trem.

ISOLDA.
ISOLDE.
Quick, say without fear!
Frei sag's oh-ne Furcht!
BRANGÆNA.
BRANGÄNE.
With courteous phrase he foiled my will.
Mit höf'-schen Wor-ten wich er aus.
ISOLDA.
ISOLDE.
But when you bade him hi-ther?
Doch als du deut-lich mahntest?
When I had straightway bid him come, where'er he stood, he said to me, he tru-ly served but thee, the pearl of wo-man-hood; if he un-heed-ed left the helm how could he pi-lot the
Da ich zur Stell' ihn zu dir rief: wo er auch steh', so sag-te er, ge-treu-lich dien' er ihr, der Frau-en höch-ster Ehr'; liess' er das Steu-er jetzt zur Stund', wie lenkt' er si-cher den
p
cresc.
mf
sf
dim.
dolce
tr
dim.

Poco ritenuto.
Etwas zurückhaltend.
ISOLDA (bitterly).
ISOLDE (schmerzlich bitter).
(molto steso)
(sehr gedehnt)
ship in surety to King Mark? "How could he pi-lot the ship in
Kiel zu König Marke's Land? „Wie lenkt' er sicher den Kiel zu
più p
Molto vivace, come prima.
Wieder sehr lebhaft.
(shrill and vehemently)
(grell und heftig)
surety to King Mark!" And wait on him with
König Marke's Land!" Den Zins ihm aus-zu-
cresc.
were-gild from isle of Ire-land won!
zah-len, den er aus Ir-land zog!
più f
ff
BRANGÆNA.
BRANGÄNE.
As I gave out thy message and in thy ve-ry
Auf dei-ne eig'-nen Wor-te, als ich ihm die ent-
mf
ISOLDA.
ISOLDE.
words, thus spoke his henchman Kur-ve-nal Heard I not ev'-ry
bot, liess sei-nen Die-ner Kur-we-nal Den hab' ich wohl ver-

sentence? it all has reached my ear. If thou hast learnt my dis-
nommen, kein Wort, das mir entging. Er-fuh-rest du mei-ne
grace, now hear
Schmach, nun hö-
too whence it has grown.
re, was sie mir schuf.
Con molto moto, vacillando il tempo.
Sehr bewegt und wechselvoll im Zeitmass.
How
Wie
scoffingly they sing a-bout me! Quick-ly could I re-quite them!
lachend sie mir Lieder sin-gen, wohl könnt' auch ich er-wi-dern!
Più moderato.
Mässiger.
What of the boat so bare and frail, that floated by our
Von ei-nem Kahn, der klein und arm an Irlands Kü-sten
poco rall.
cresc.
dim.
più f

shore? What of the brok - en stri - cken man, feebly ex - tend - ed
schwamm, da-rinnen krank ein sie - cher Mann e-lend im Ster-ben
p
più p
there? I-sol-da's art he glad-ly owned; with herbs, sim-ples
lag. I-sol-de's Kunst ward ihm be-kannt, mit Heil-sal-ben
riten.
and healing salves the wounds from which he suf - fered she nursed in skil-ful
und Balsam-saft der Wun-de, die ihn plag - te, ge-treu-lich pflag sie
riten.
p
più p
dim.
a tempo
Sempre più animato.
Immer belebter.
wise. Though "Tan - tris" the name that he took un - to him, as
da. Der „Tan - tris" mit sor - gender List sich nannte, als
a tempo
pp
p
cresc.
Più mosso.
Schneller.
"Tris - tan" I - sol - da quick - ly knew him, when in the
„Tri - stan" I - sold' ihn bald er - kann - te, da in des
fp
p

sick man's keen blade she perceiv'd a notch had been made, wherein did
Müss' - gen Schwer - te ei - ne Scharte sie ge - wahr - te, darin ge -
fit a splin - ter brok - en in Morold's head, the man - gled
nau sich fügt' ein Split - ter, den einst im Haupt des I - ren -
p
cresc.
Vivace.
Schnell.
token sent home in ha - tred rare: this hand did find it there.
ritter, zum Hohn ihr heimgesandt, mit kund'ger Hand sie fand.
f
ff
I heard a voice from dis - tance
Da schrie's mir auf aus tief - stem
dim.
dim!
Grund!
ff
With the sword in
Mit dem hel - len

hand I came to him.
Schwert ich vor ihm stund,
Full well I
an ihm, dem
dim.
poco rallent. ritenuto
willed to slay him, for Mo - rold's death to pay him.
Ü - ber - fre - chen, Herrn Mo - rold's Tod zu rä - chen.
cresc.
ff
p
dolce
weich
Molto moderato.
Sehr mässig.
But from his sick - bed he looked
Von sei - nem La - ger blickt' er
p
up,—
her,—
not at the sword, not at my
nicht auf das Schwert, nicht auf die
Molto ritardando.
Sehr zurückhaltend.
arm,—
Hand,—
his eyes on mine were fast - en'd,
er sah mir in die Au - gen.
molto espressivo e dolce
sehr ausdrucksvoll u. zart
p molto cresc.
ff

and his fee - ble - ness soft - en'd my heart; the sword
Seines E - len - des jam - mer - te mich; das Schwert
cresc.
Lento.
Langsam.
Moderato.
Mässig.
dropp'd from my fingers! Though Mo - rold's steel had maim'd him, to
ich liess es fal - len! Die Mo - rold schlug, die Wun - de, sie
health a - gain I re - claim'd him; when he had homeward wended my e - motion
heilt' ich, dass er ge - sun - de, und heim nach Hau - se keh - re, mit dem Blick mich
più p
Più mosso.
Schneller.
Brangæna.
Brangäne.
then might be ended! O wond - rous!
nicht mehr beschwe - re! O Wun - der!
più p
Why could I not see this? The guest I some - time helped to nurse? His
Wo hatt' ich die Au - gen? Der Gast, den einst ich pfle - gen half? Sein
Ancora più mosso.
Immer noch beschleunigend.
Isolda.
Isolde.
dim.
cresc.

praise brisk - ly they sing now:— "Bra - vo, our brave Tris - tan!" — He was that distress - ful man.— A thou - - sand pro - tes - ta - - tions of truth and love he prat - ed! Hear now how a knight
Lob hör - test du e - ben:— „Hei! unser Held Tri - stan!" Der war je - ner traur'ge Mann.— Er schwur mit tau - - send Ei - - den mir ew' - - gen Dank und Treu - e! Nun hör', wie ein Held
Con molto fuoco.
Sehr feurig.
molto cresc.
meno f
dim.
cresc.

feal - ty knows!
Ei - de hält!
ff
f
ff
dim.
Whenas Tan - tris un - for-bid - den he'd
Den als Tan - tris un - erkannt ich ent-
p
left me, as Tris - tan bold - ly back he came; in state - ly
las - sen, als Tri - stan kehrt er kühn zu - rück; auf stol - zem
fp
f
p
ship from which in pride Ire - land's heir - ess in marriage he
Schiff, von ho - hem Bord, Ir - lands Er - bin begehrt' er zur
f
p
cresc.
Poco steso.
Etwas gedehnt.
rallent.
Vivo.
Schnell.
asked, for Mark, the Cornish monarch, his kinsman worn and old.
Eh' für Kornwalls mü - den Kö - nig, für Mar - ke, sei - nen Ohm.
ff
dim.
p
p cresc.

In Mo - rold's life - time dared an - y have
Da Mo - rold leb - te, wer hätt' es ge -
dreamed to of - fer us such an in - sult? For the
wagt, uns je sol - che Schmach zu bie - ten? Für der
tax - pay - ing Corn - ish prince to presume to court Ire - land's
zins - pflicht' - gen Kor - nen Für - sten um Ir - lands Kro - ne zu
cresc.
poco rallent.
prin - cess! Ah, woe is
wer - ben! Ach, we - he
Moderato.
Müssig.
me! I it was who for my - self did shape this
mir! Ich ja war's, die heim - lich selbst die Schmach sich
dim.
più p

Animato.
Belebt.
shame! With death - deal - ing sword should I have stabbed him;
schuf! Das rä - chen - de Schwert, statt es zu schwin - gen,
fp
molto riten.
Ancora più riten.
Noch mehr zurückhaltend.
weak - ly it escaped me! Now serf - dom
macht - los liess ich's fal - len! Nun dien' ich
f
ff
dim.
p
Vivo, come prima.
Wieder schnell.
I have shaped me!
dem Va - sal - len!
p
molto cresc.
ff
BRANGÆNA.
BRANGÄNE.
When fealty, peace and friend - - ship were sworn
Da Friede, Sühn' und Freund - - schaft von Al -
meno f
f
p
molto cresc.
by both the na - tions, what feast - ing we kept that day! How
len ward be - schwo - ren, wir freu - ten uns All' des Tag's; wie
dim.

could I have thought that thou wouldst suf - fer thus?
ahn-te mir da, dass dir es Kum-mer schüf'?
ISOLDA.
ISOLDE.
acceler.
p molto cresc.
O vis - - ion blind - ed!
O blin - - de Au - gen!
Veiled per-cep - tion! Spi - - rit weak! Des-pair - ing
Blö - - de Her - zen! Zah - - mer Muth, ver-zag - tes
silence! And bold-ly Tristan's tongue could boast of what I kept con-
Schweigen! Wie an-ders prahlte Tri - stan aus, was ich verschlos - sen
dim.
più p
Meno mosso.
Mässiger.
cealed! A wo - - man's si - lence saved his
hielt! Die schwei gend ihm das Le - ben

life, from foe - - men's ven - geance it ward - - ed him; the

*gab, vor Fein - - des Ra - - che ihn schwei - - gend barg; was*

*p* *pp*

(più appassionato)

*(steigernd)*

*acceler.*

hid - den help he owed to her

*stumm ihr Schutz zum Heil ihm schuf,*

*acceler.*

*p* *sfp cresc.*

**Allegro.**

***Schnell.***

with her— thus doth he praise!

*mit ihr— gab er es preis!*

*f*

With what pride this he - - ro high,

*Wie sieg - - prangend, heil und hehr,*

*f* tr

light at heart, point - ed me out!

*laut und hell wies er auf mich:*

*fp* *fp* *fp* *cresc.* *f* *dim.*

Poco più moderato.
Etwas mässiger.
"A prize be - hold, my lord and
„Das wär' ein Schatz, mein Herr und
p
più p
dolce
Ancora più moderato.
Noch mässiger.
King; she'd make a mo - del queen. From Ire - land's
Ohm; wie dünkt euch die zur Eh'? Die schmu - cke
p dolce
Animando.
Belebend.
court I'll bring the bride; the road and way full well I know; a
I - rin hol' ich her; mit Steg und We - gen wohl - be - kannt, ein
cresc.
Sempre più animato.
Immer belebter.
word, and I'll to Ire - land go; I - sold' for you I'll
Wink, ich flieg' nach I - ren - land; I - sol - de, die ist
cap - ture: I
eu - er! mir
acceler.
f
più f

poco riten.
Allegro molto.
Sehr schnell.
hail the task with rapture!"
lacht das A - ben - teu-er!"
Curse him, the vil - lain!
Fluch dir, Ver - ruch - ter!
Curse
Fluch
on his head!
dei - nem Haupt!
Ven - geance!
Ra - che!
Death!
Tod!

Death for me too!
Tod uns Bei - den!
BRANGÆNA (throwing herself on Isolda with eager tenderness).
BRANGÄNE (mit ungestümer Zärtlichkeit sich auf Isolde stürzend).
I - sol - da! La - dy! Lov'd one!
O Sü - sse! Trau - te! Theu - re!
ff
Fair - est! Sweet per - fec - tion!
Hol - de! Gold' - ne Her - rin!
(She gradually draws Isolda to the couch.)
(Sie zieht Isolde allmählich nach dem Ruhebett.)
Mis - tress rar - est!
Lieb' I - sol - de!
decresc. poco a poco
Hear me! Come now! Sit thee
Hör' mich! Kom - me! Setz' dich

Sempre con molto moto.
Immer noch sehr bewegt.
here! What a whim! what causeless rail - ing! How came you so wrong-mind - ed and by mere fan - cies blind - ed? Sir Tris-tan gives thee Corn - wall's king - dom; then, were he erst thy debt - or, how could he e'er reward thee bet - ter? His no - ble un - cle serves he so; think
her! Wel - cher Wahn! Welch' eit - les Zür - nen! Wie magst du dich be - thö - ren, nicht hell zu seh'n noch hö - ren? Was je Herr Tri - stan dir ver - dank - te, sag; konnt' er's hö - her loh - nen, als mit der herr - lichsten der Kro - nen? So dient' er treu dem ed - len Ohm; dir
p
mf
cresc.

too what a gift on thee he'd be-stow! With honour unequalled all he's
gab er der Welt be-gehr-lichsten Lohn: dem eig'nen Er-be, echt und
p
p
heir to at thy feet he now would show - - - er, to
e-del, ent - sagt' er zu dei-nen Fü - - - ssen, als
p
cresc.
p cresc.
(Isolda turns away.)
(Isolde wendet sich ab.)
form thee a queen - ly dow-er!
Kö - ni-gin dich zu grü-ssen!
f
p
ff
dim.
If wife he'd make thee un-to King
Und warb er Mar - ke dir zum Ge-
p
p
p
Mark, why wert thou in this wise com-plain - ing? Is he not worth thy
mahl, wie woll-test du die Wahl doch schel ten, muss er nicht werth dir
p

gaining? Of roy - - al race and mild of mood, who
gel - ten? Von ed - - ler Art und mildem Muth, wer
espressivo
ausdrucksvoll
p
p sempre legato
pas - - ses King Mark in might and pow'r? If a
gli - - che dem Mann an Macht und Glanz? Dem ein
cresc.
p
no - ble knight like Tris - tan serves him, who could not
hehr - ster Held so treu - lich dient, wer möch - te
p
p
cresc.
but feel e - lat - - ed, so fair -
sein Glück nicht thei - - len, als Gat -
p
p
p
cresc.
ly to be mat - - - ed?
tin bei ihm wei - - - len?
f
dim.
p
ff

ISOLDA (staring before her).
*ISOLDE (starr vor sich hinblickend).*

Glo - - - - - - - rious knight! And
*Un - - - - - - - ge - minnt den*

p p

I ___ must near him love - - less ev - - - er
*hehr - - - sten Mann stets ___ mir nah' zu*

p cresc.

lan - - - - guish! ___ How can I sup - port this anguish?
*se - - - - hen! ___ wie könnt' ich die Qual be - ste - hen?*

f ff sf f

BRANGÆNA.
*BRANGÄNE.*

What's this, my la - dy? (♩. = 𝅗𝅥) love - - less thou? ___
*Was meinst du Ar - ge? Un - - ge - minnt? ___*

f p dolce

(She approaches Isolda with cajoling and caresses.)
*(Sie nähert sich schmeichelnd und kosend Isolden.)*

Where ___
*Wo ___*

p

*espressivo*
*ausdrucksvoll*

lives there a man that would not love thee? Who could see
leb - te der Mann, der dich nicht lieb - te? der I - sol -
I - sol - da and not sink at once in - to
- den säh', und in I - sol - den se - lig nicht
dolcissimo
sehr weich
bond - age blest? And e'en if it could be
ganz ver - ging? Doch, der dir er - ko - ren,
dim.
an - y were cold, did an - y ma - gic draw him
wär' er so kalt, zög' ihn von dir ein Zau - ber
thence, I'd bring the false one back to bond -
ab, den Bö - sen wüsst' ich bald zu bin -
dim.
più p
pp

- - - - age and bind him in links of
- - - - den; ihn bann - te der Min - - - ne
poco a poco cresc.
(Secretly and confidentially approaching close to Isolda.)
(Mit geheimnissvoller Zutraulichkeit ganz nah zu Isolden.)
love.
Macht.
Mind-est thou not thy mother's
Kennst du der Mutter Künste
f dim. più p
pp
arts? Think you that she who'd mastered those would have
nicht? Wähnst du, die Al - les klug er - wägt, oh - ne
sent me o'er the sea without as - sis - tance for thee?
Rath in fremdes Land hätt' sie mit dir mich ent - sandt?
Poco più lento.
Etwas langsamer.
ISOLDA (darkly).
ISOLDE (düster).
My mother's rede I mind a - right, and highly her magic arts I
Der Mut - ter Rath gemahnt mich recht; will - kom - men preis' ich ih - re

hold: — Vengeance they wreak for wrongs, — rest give to wounded
Kunst: — Rache für den Verrath, — Ruh' in der Noth dem
p cresc. f pp più p pp
Brangæna.
Brangäne.
spirits! — Yon casket hither bear! It holds — a balm — for
Herzen! — Den Schrein dort bring' mir her! Er birgt, — was heil — dir
p p
Poco animando.
Etwas belebend.
thee. — (She brings forward a small golden coffer, opens it and points out its contents.) Thy
frommt. — (Sie holt eine kleine goldne Truhe herbei, öffnet sie und deutet auf ihren Inhalt.) So
p poco cresc. p dolce
mother placed inside it her subtle magic potions:
reih-te sie die Mut-ter, die mächt'gen Zau-ber-tränke:
p
There's salve for sickness or for wounds, and antidotes for deadly
Für Weh' und Wunden Bal-sam hier, für bö-se Gif-te Ge-gen-
p

(She takes out a small flask.)
(Sie zieht ein Fläschchen hervor.)
(Moderato.)
a tempo (Mässig.)
drugs.
gift.
The help - ful - lest draught I hold it here.
Den hehr - sten Trank, ich halt' ihn hier.
molto rallent.
a tempo
p dolce
f
p dolce
Isolda.
Isolde.
Not so, I know a bet - ter.
Du irrst, ich kenn' ihn bes - ser;
più p
pp
I made a mark to know it a - gain.
ein star - kes Zei - chen schnitt ich ihm ein.
p
(She seizes a bottle and shows it.)
(Sie ergreift ein Fläschchen und zeigt es.)
cresc poco a poco
This draught 'tis, I would
Der Trank ist's, der mir
ff
p

Presto. (She has risen from the couch and listens with rising dread to the cries of the seamen.)
Schnell. (Sie hat sich vom Ruhebett erhoben und vernimmt mit wachsendem Schrecken den Ruf des Schiffsvolks.)
drain.
taugt!
Brangæna.
Brangäne.
(She recoils in horror.)
(Sie weicht entsetzt zurück.)
The dead - - ly draught!
Der To - - des - trank!
1st Tenor.
1. Tenor.
Ho! heave ho! heave ho! heave ho! heave
Ho! he! ha! he! ho! he! ha! he!
Seamen (without).
Schiffsvolk (aussen).
1st Bass.
1. Bass.
Re - duce the sail! The mainsail in!
Am Un - ter - mast die Se - gel ein!
Isolda.
Isolde.
Our jour - - ney has been
Das deu - - tet schnel - le
1st Tenor.
1. Tenor.
ho! heave ho!
ho! he! ho!
2nd Tenor.
2. Tenor.
Re - duce the sail! The mainsail in!
Am Un - ter - mast die Se - gel ein!
1st and 2nd Bass.
1. u. 2. Bäss.
Ho! heave ho! heave ho! heave ho hey!
Ho! he! ha! he! ho! he! ha! he!

swift!
Fahrt!
Woe's me! Near_ to the
Weh mir! Na he das
(strepitoso)
Scene IV. | Vierte Scene.
(Through the curtains enters Kurvenal boisterously.)
(Durch die Vorhänge tritt mit Ungestüm Kurwenal herein.)
Vivace.
Lebhaft.
KURVENAL.
KURWENAL.
land! Up! Up! ye
Land! Auf! Auf! Ihr
la - - - - - - - dies!
Frau - - - - - - - en!
Look a-lert! Straight be-stir you! Loi-ter not; here is the land!
Frisch und froh! Rasch ge-rü-stet! Fer-tig nun, hur-tig und flink!
dim.
cresc.

To dame I - - - sol_da says the ser_vant of
Und Frau I - - - sol_den sollt' ich sa_gen von
cresc.
p dolce
Tris - tan, our he - ro true: Be - hold, our flag is fly - ing!
Held Tri_stan, mei_nem Herrn: Vom Mast der Freu_de Flag - ge,
un poco cresc.
it wav - eth land_wards a - loft; in Mark's an -
sie we - he lu - stig ins Land; in Mar - ke's
ces - tral cas - - - - - - tle may our ap -
Kö - nigs_schlos - - - - - se mach' sie ihr
più cresc.
proach be seen. So Dame I - sold' he prays to
Nah'n be - kannt. Drum Frau I - sol - de bät' er,
tr

hast - en, for land straight to pre -
ei - len, fürs Land sich zu be -
ff
ff
pare her, that thi - ther he may bear
rei - - - - - - ten, dass er sie könnt' ge - lei - - -
p
cresc.
f
ff
her.
ten.
Moderato.
Mässig.
ISOLDA (who has at first started and trembled at the message, now composed and dignified).
ISOLDE (nachdem sie zuerst bei der Meldung in Schauer zusammengefahren, gefasst und mit Würde).
My
Herrn
ff
greet - ing take un - to your lord and tell him what I
Tri - stan brin - ge mei - nen Gruss, und meld' ihm, was ich
p
p

say now: Should he as-sist to land me and to King Mark would he hand me, un-
sa-ge. Sollt' ich zur Seit' ihm ge-hen, vor Kö-nig Mar-ke zu ste-hen, nicht
mf
p
meet and un-seem-ly were his act, the while my par-don was not
möcht' es nach Zucht und Fug ge-scheh'n, em-pfing' ich Süh-ne nicht zu
p
p
won for tres-pass black and base:
vor für un-ge-sühn-te Schuld:
so bid him seek my
drum such' er mei-ne
f dim.
pp
ten.
p
(Kurvenal makes a defiant gesture.)
(Kurwenal macht eine trotzige Gebärde.)
(con impeto)
(mit Steigerung)
grace.
Huld.
Now mark me well:
Du mer-ke wohl
f
ff
ff dim.
this message take!
und meld' es gut!
Nought will I yet pre-pare me, that he to land may
Nicht woll' ich mich be-rei-ten, ans Land ihn zu be-
f
mf

(moderando)
(sich mässigend)
bear me, I will not by him be landed, nor unto King Mark be
gleiten; nicht werd' ich zur Seit' ihm gehen, vor König Marke zu
handed ere granting forgiveness and forgetfulness, which 'tis seemly he should
stehen, begehrte Vergessen und Vergeben nach Zucht und Fug er nicht zu-
seek. For all his trespass base I tender him my
vor für ungebüsste Schuld:— die böt' ihm meine
KURVENAL.
KURWENAL.
grace. Be assured, I'll bear your words; we'll see what he will
Huld! Sicher wisst, das sag' ich ihm; nun harrt, wie er mich
Molto mosso.
Sehr bewegt.
(Isolda hastens to Brangaena and embraces her vehemently.)
(Isolde eilt auf Brangäne zu und umarmt sie heftig.)
ISOLDA.
ISOLDE.
say! (He goes off quickly.)
hört! (Er geht schnell zurück.)
Now fare-
Nun leb'
p molto cresc.

well, Bran - gæ - - - - na! Greet ev' - ry
wohl, Bran - gä - - - - ne! Grüss' mir die
ff
f
p
poco riten.
Presto. BRANGÆNA.
Schnell. BRANGÄNE.
one, greet my fa - ther and mo_ther! What now? What
Welt, grü - sse mir Va - ter und Mut_ter! Was ist? Was
f
dim.
p
p
f
f
Moderato e ritenuto.
Mässig und zurückhaltend.
mean'st thou? Would_est thou flee? Oh where must I then fol_low?
sinnst du? Woll_test du flieh'n? Wo_hin soll ich dir fol_gen?
f
f
f dim.
(Isolda suddenly checks herself.)
(Isolde fasst sich schnell.)
ISOLDA.
ISOLDE.
Here I re - main: heard you not?
Hör_test du nicht? Hier bleib' ich,
p
più p
pp
p
Tris - tan well will I wait for. I trust in thee to aid in
Tri - stan will ich er - war - ten. Ge - treu be_folg' was ich be -
p
pp
pp
p

this: pre - pare the true cup of peace;— thou
fehl': den Süh - ne - trank rü - - ste schnell;— du
p
p
p
(Isolda takes out the flask from the coffer.)
(Isolde entnimmt dem Schrein das Fläschchen.)
Brangæna.
Brangäne.
Isolda.
Isolde.
3
mind'st how it is made? What mean-est thou? This is it! From the flask go
weisst, den ich dir wies? Und wel-chen Trank? Die - sen Trank! In die gold'-ne
p
cresc.
ff
dim.
Prèsto.
Schnell.
pour this phil-tre out; yon gold gob-let'twill fill.
Scha - le giess' ihn aus; ge - füllt fasst sie ihn ganz.
p
f
Isolda.
Isolde.
Brangæna (taking the flask in terror).
Brangäne (voll Grausen das Fläschchen empfangend).
Wilt— thou be
Sei— du mir
Trust I my wits?
Trau' ich dem Sinn?
più f
ff
dim.

true?
treu!
Him who be - trayed!
Wer mich be - trog.
The draught — for whom?
Den Trank — für wen?
Tris - - - tan?
Tri - - - stan?
p
f
dim.
ISOLDA.
ISOLDE.
Truce he'll drink with me!
Trin - ke mir Süh - - - ne!
p cresc.
BRANGÆNA (throwing herself at Isolda's feet).
BRANGÄNE (zu Isolde's Füssen stürzend).
O hor - - ror!
Ent - set - - zen!
Pit - - y thy hand - maid!
Scho - - ne mich Ar - me!
ff
f
ff
f
ff
ISOLDA (molto violente).
ISOLDE (sehr heftig).
Pit - - - - - y thou me, false - heart - ed
Scho - - - - - ne du mich, un - - treu - e
più f

maid!
Magd!
Mind-est thou not my mo-ther's
Kennst du der Mut-ter Kün-ste
ff
Poco a poco ritenuto.
Allmählich etwas zurückhaltend.
arts?
nicht?
Think you that she who'd mas-ter'd those
Wähnst du, die Al-les klug er-wägt,
would have sent thee o'er the
oh-ne Rath in frem-des
dim.
p
sea with no as-sis-tance for me?
Land hätt' sie mit dir mich ent-sandt?
A salve for
Für Weh' und
dim.
pp
p
sick-ness doth she of-fer,
Wun-den gab sie Bal-sam,
and an-ti-dotes for dead-ly
für bö-se Gif-te Ge-gen-
p
p
p

Lento e steso.
*Gedehnt und langsam.*

drugs: for deep - est grief and woe su -
*gift: für tief - stes Weh, für höch - stes*

pp cresc.

Più mosso come prima.
*Wieder bewegter.*

preme gave__ she the draught of death.
*Leid gab__ sie den To - des trank.*

f ff trem. p

Lento.
*Langsam.*
BRANGÆNA (almost beside herself).
*BRANGÄNE (kaum ihrer mächtig).*

Let Death now give her thanks! O deep - est
*Der Tod nun sag' ihr Dank! O tief - stes*

più p rallent. pp pp

ISOLDA.
*ISOLDE.*
poco accel. molto acceler.

Now wilt thou o - bey? Wilt thou be true?
*Gehorchst du mir nun? Bist du mir treu?*

BRANGÆNA.
*BRANGÄNE.*

grief! O woe su - preme! The draught?
*Weh! O höch - stes Leid! Der Trank?*

KURVENAL (entering.)
*KURWENAL (eintretend).*

Sir
*Herr*

poco accel. molto acceler.
p poco cresc. molto cresc.

(Brangæna rises, terrified and confused. Isolda strives with a mighty effort to compose herself.)
*(Brangäne erhebt sich erschrocken und verwirrt. Isolde sucht mit furchtbarer Anstrengung sich zu fassen.)*

Vivace.
Lebhaft.
Poco ritenuto.
Etwas zurückhaltend.
Tris - tan!
Tri - stan!
f
più f
ff
dim.
ISOLDA (to Kurvenal).
ISOLDE (zu Kurwenal).
Sir Tris - tan
Herr Tri - stan
may ap -
tre - te
più p
p

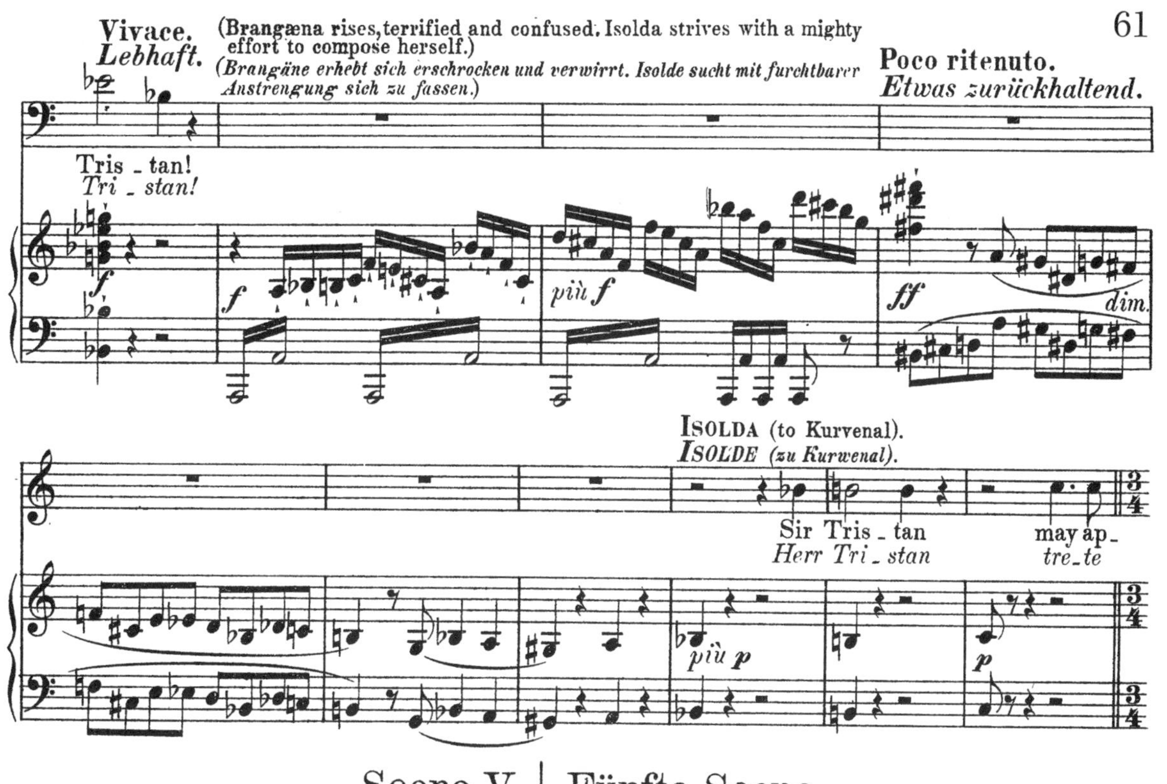

## Scene V. | Fünfte Scene.

(Kurvenal retires again. Brangæna, scarcely mistress of herself, turns towards the back. Isolda, summoning all her powers to meet the crisis, walks slowly and with effort to the couch, leaning on the head of which she then stands, her eyes fixed on the entrance.)
*(Kurwenal geht wieder zurück. Brangäne, kaum ihrer mächtig, wendet sich in den Hintergrund. Isolde, ihr ganzes Gefühl zur Entscheidung zusammenfassend, schreitet langsam, mit grosser Haltung, dem Ruhebett zu, auf dessen Kopfende sich stützend, sie den Blick fest dem Eingange zuwendet.)*

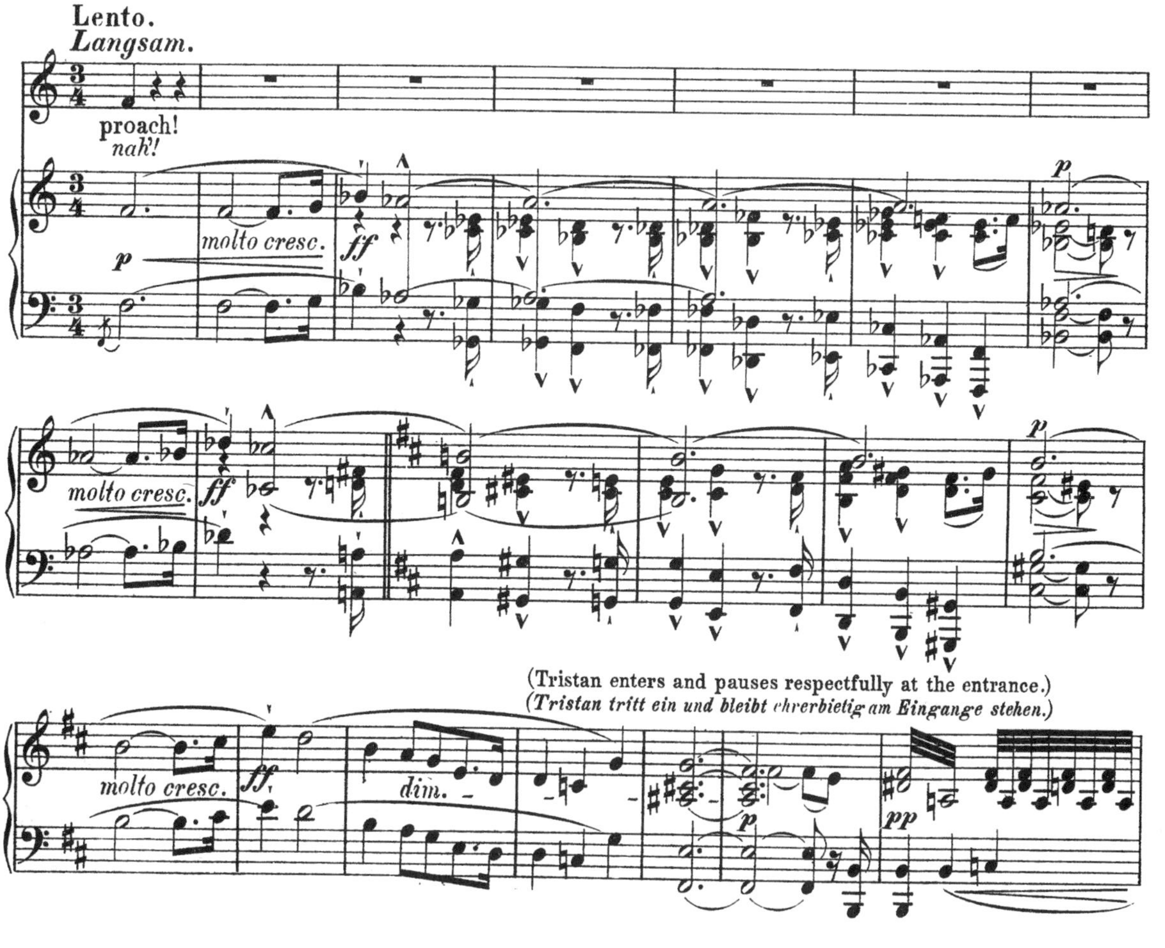

Lento.
Langsam.
proach!
nah!
p
molto cresc.
ff
p
molto cresc.
ff
p
(Tristan enters and pauses respectfully at the entrance.)
(Tristan tritt ein und bleibt ehrerbietig am Eingange stehen.)
molto cresc.
ff
dim.
p
pp

(Isolda is in dreadful emotion sunk in his contemplation.)
(Isolde ist mit furchtbarer Aufregung in seinen Anblick versunken.)
cresc.
sf
mf
p
f
p
cresc.
f
ff
TRISTAN.
TRISTAN.
Demand, la-dy, what you will.
Begehrt, Her-rin, was ihr wünscht.
p
p
sf
p
ISOLDA.
ISOLDE.
While know-ing not what my de-mand is, wert thou a-fraid still to ful-
Wüss-test du nicht, was ich be-geh-re, da doch die Furcht, mir's zu er-
p
fil it, flee-ing my pre-sence thus?
fül-len, fern mei-nem Blick dich hielt?
TRISTAN.
TRISTAN.
Hon-our
Ehrfurcht
p
p

ISOLDA.
ISOLDE.
held me in awe. Scant hon - our hast thou shewn to-wards
hielt mich in Acht. Der Eh - re we - nig bo - test du
tenuto
gehalten
p cresc.
me; for un - a - bash'd thou hast withheld o - bedience un-to my call.
mir; mit off'nem Hohn ver-wehr-test du Ge - hor-sam meinem Ge - bot.
TRISTAN.
TRISTAN.
O
Ge -
mf
p
ISOLDA.
ISOLDE.
But lit - tle I owe thy lord, methinks,
So dankt' ich Ge - rin-ges dei-nem Herrn,
bedience 'twas for - bade me to come.
hor-sam ein - zig hielt mich in Bann.
p
p
if he al - lows ill man-ners un-to his own promised bride!
rieth dir sein Dienst Un - sit - te ge-gen sein ei - gen Ge-mahl?
TRISTAN.
TRISTAN.
In our
Sit - te
ff
p

land it is the law that he who fet - ches home the bride should stay a - far - from
lehrt, wo ich ge - lebt: zur Braut-fahrt der Braut - wer - ber mei - de fern die
cresc.
mf
dim.
ISOLDA.
ISOLDE.
TRISTAN.
TRISTAN.
her. On what ac - count? 'Tis the cus - tom!
Braut. Aus wel - cher Sorg? Fragt die Sit - te!
p
f
p
pp
ISOLDA.
ISOLDE.
If you're so care - ful, my lord Tris - tan, one oth - - - er
Da du so sitt - sam, mein Herr Tri - stan, auch ei - - - ner
p
tenuto
gehalten
poco cresc.
custom can you not learn? Of en - nemies friends make: for e - vil
Sit - te sei nun ge - mahnt: den Feind dir zu süh - nen, soll er als
sf
sf
p
TRISTAN.
TRISTAN.
ISOLDA.
ISOLDE.
acts a - mends make. Who is my foe? Find in thy
Freund dich rüh - men. Und wel - chen Feind? Frag' dei - ne
cresc.
sf
molto cresc.

TRISTAN.
*TRISTAN.*

fears! Blood-guilt gets bet-ween us. That was ab-
*Furcht! Blut-schuld schwebt zwi-schen uns. Die ward ge-*

ff f ff pp p

ISOLDA.
*ISOLDE.*

'solved. Not bet-ween us!
*sühnt. Nicht zwi-schen uns!*

TRISTAN.
*TRISTAN.*

In op-en field, 'fore all the
*Im off'nen Feld, vor al-lem*

f ff p f

Poco più mosso, ma moderato.
*Etwas bewegter, doch mässig.*

ISOLDA.
*ISOLDE.*

folk our old feud was a-bandoned. 'Twas not there I held
*Volk ward Ur-feh-de ge-schwo-ren. Nicht da war's, wo ich*

f p

Tan-tris hid and Tris-tan in my pow'r. He stood there
*Tan-tris barg, wo Tri-stan mir ver-fiel. Da stand er*

p dolce
dolce
*weich*

brawn-y, bright and brave; but in his
*herr-lich, hehr und heil; doch was er*

p molto cresc.

truce I took no part:— my tongue its si_lence had learnt.
schwur, das schwur ich nicht:— zu schweigen hatt' ich ge_lernt.
Ani_
Be_
When in chamber'd still_ness sick he lay,
Da in stil_ler Kam_mer krank er lag,
mando.
lebend.
with the sword I stood be_fore him, stern:
mit dem Schwer_te stumm ich vor ihm stund:
si_ _ _ lent my lips,
schwieg da mein Mund,
mo_ _ tion_less my
bannt' ich mei_ne
Molto vivace.
Sehr lebhaft.
hand·— but that which my hand and lips once had
Hand;— doch was einst mit Hand und Mund ich ge_
f
p
mf
cresc.
più f
fp

vowed, I swore in stealth to adhere to. Lo!
lobt, das schwur ich schweigend zu hal_ten. Nun
ff
pp
Più moderato.
Wieder mässiger.
TRISTAN.
TRISTAN.
acceler.
now my de_sire I'm near to. What hast thou sworn?
will ich des Ei_des wal_ten. Was schwurt ihr, Frau?
acceler.
p
pp
p
p cresc.
ISOLDA (quickly).
ISOLDE (lebhafter).
riten.
TRISTAN (quietly). Più vivo. ISOLDA (animated).
TRISTAN (mässig). Lebhafter. ISOLDE (lebhaft).
Ven_geance for Morold! Mind'st thou that? Dare you to
Ra_che für Morold! Müht euch die? Wagst du zu
riten.
f
p
cresc.
flout me?_
höh_nen?_
Was he not my be_
An_ge_lobt war er
ff
dim.
p
throthed, that no_ble I_rish knight? For his sword a
mir, der heh_re I_ren_held; sei_ne Waf_fen
dolce
p

blessing I sought; for me only he fought.
hatt' ich geweiht; für mich zog er zum Streit.
cresc.
f
Ancora più animando.
Noch etwas mehr belebend.
When he was murdered my honour fell; in that heart felt
Da er gefallen, fiel meine Ehr'; in des Herzens
fp
p
cresc.
mis'ry my vow was framed: if no man re-
Schwere schwur ich den Eid: würd' ein Mann den
fp
cresc.
mained to right it, I, a maid, must needs re-
Mord nicht sühnen, wollt' ich Magd mich dess' erten.
f
Poco più moderato.
Etwas mässiger.
quite it.—
Weak and maimed when might was mine,
kühnen.—
Siech und matt in meiner Macht,
p
trem.
sf
p
p

**Più animato.**
*Belebter.*

why at thy death did I pause,
*wa_rum ich dich da nicht schlug,*

rallent.

*f* *dim.*

**Più moderato.**
*Mässiger.*
(ritenuto)
*(zurückhaltend)*

**Animando.**
*Belebend.*

thou now shalt know the se_cret cause:_ Thy hurts I tend_ed
*das sag' dir selbst mit leichtem Fug:_ Ich pflag des Wun_den,*

*p* *p* *cresc.*

that, when sick_ness end_ed, thou shouldst fall by some man, as I_
*dass den heil Ge_sun_den rä_chend schlü_ge der Mann, der I_*

*f*

sol_da's re_venge should plan._
*sol_den ihn ab_ge_wann._*

But
*Dein*

*f* *f* *dim.* *p*

**Moderato.**
*Mässig.*
(poco steso)
*(etwas gedehnt)*

now at_tempt thy fate to fore_tell_ me: If their
*Los nun sel_ber magst du dir sa_gen! Da die*

*pp* *p* *cresc.*

friend-ship true all men do sell — thee, what foe can seek to
Män-ner sich all' ihm ver-tra-gen, wer muss nun Tri-stan
ff
f
fell thee?
schla-gen?
ff
3
3
rallent.
dim.
Lento.
Langsam.
TRISTAN (pale and gloomy).
TRISTAN (bleich und düster).
If thou so lov'dst this lord, then lift once more my
War Mo-rold dir so werth, nun wie-der nimm das
p
più p
pp
pp
(He hands her his sword.)
(Er reicht ihr sein Schwert dar.)
sword, nor from thy pur-pose re-frain; let the weap-on not fall a-
Schwert, und führ' es si-cher und fest, dass du nicht dir's ent-fal-len
cresc.
p
f
p
Poco più mosso,
Etwas bewegter.
ISOLDA.
ISOLDE.
gain!
lässt!
That scarce would
Wie sorgt' ich
pp

suit thy lord and mas_ter: how, think you, would King Mark ab_solve me if slain by me his
schlecht um dei_nen Her_ren; was wür_de Kö_nig Mar_ke sa_gen, er_schlüg' ich ihm den
p
ser_vant were who won him king_dom and crown, the knight of high re_nown?
be_sten Knecht, der Kron' und Land ihm ge_wann, den al_ler_treu_sten Mann?
dim.
p
Think'st thou thy chief so char_y of thanks, when thou hast brought his bride from the
Dünkt dich so we_nig, was er dir dankt, bringst du die I_rin ihm als
p
west, that he'd not curse thy kil_ler, proud woo_er, who bore her in hand as
Braut, dass er nicht schöl_te, schlüg' ich den Wer_ber, der Ur_feh_de-Pfand so
p
sf dim.
p
rallent.
Più lento.
Langsamer.
pledge of peace to his land? Put up thy sword which once I
treu ihm lie_fert zur Hand? Wah_re dein Schwert! Da einst ich's
p
p
p
cresc.

acceler.
rallent.
swung, when venge - ful ran_cour my bo_som wrung,
schwang, als mir die Ra_che im Bu_sen rang,
fp cresc.
ff
when thy mas_ter_ful eyes did ask me straight whether King Mark might
als dein mes_sen_der Blick mein Bild sich stahl, ob ich Herrn Mar_ke
dimin.
p
rallent.
call_me his mate. The sword_ harmless de_scended._ Drink!
taug?_als Ge_mahl: das Schwert_ da liess ich's sinken._ Nun
più p
ff
Moderato.
Mässig.
(She signs to Brangæna, who cowers and trembles as she mo_
(Sie winkt Brangänen. Diese schaudert zusammen, schwankt und zö_
let our strife be ended!
lass uns Süh - ne trinken!
pp
fp cresc.
ves.)
gert in ihrer Bewegung.)
f dim.
espress.
pp

(Isolda urges her with more impressive gestures.)
(Isolde treibt sie mit gesteigerter Gebärde an.)
acceler.
f
cresc.
più f
Moderato. (Bragæna sets about preparing the draught.)
Mässig. (Brangäne lässt sich zur Bereitung des Trankes an.)
sf
Voices of the Sailors (without).
Stimmen des Schiffsvolkes (von aussen).
1st Tenor.
1. Tenor.
ff
Ho! heave ho! heave ho! heave ho! heave
Ho! he! ha! he! ho! he! ha! he!
1st Bass.
1. Bass.
ff
Re-duce the sail! the fore-sail in!
Am O-ber-mast die Se-gel ein!
f
6
3
ho! heave ho!
ha! he! ha!
2nd Tenor.
2. Tenor.
ff
Re-duce the sail! the fore-sail in!
Am O-ber-mast die Se-gel ein!
ff
Ho! heave ho, hey!
Ho! he! ha! he!
2nd Bass.
2. Bass.
ff
Ho! heave ho! heave ho! heave ho, hey!
Ho! he! ha! he! ho! he! ha! he!

TRISTAN (starting from his dark brooding).
TRISTAN (aus düstrem Brüten auffahrend).
Where are we?
Wo sind wir?
ISOLDA.
ISOLDE.
Near to shore!
Hart am Ziel!
ff
f
p
pp
Tris_tan, is war_fare end_ed? Hast ne'er a word to of_fer?
Tri_stan, ge_winn' ich Süh_ne? Was hast du mir zu sa_gen?
TRISTAN (darkly).
TRISTAN (finster).
Con_ceal_ment's mis_tress makes me si_lent:_
Des Schweigens Her_rin heisst mich schwei_gen:_
I know what she con_ceals, con_ceal, too, more than she knows.
fass' ich, was sie ver_schwieg, ver_schweig' ich, was sie nicht fasst.
ISOLDA (con anima).
ISOLDE (belebend).
acceler.
Thy si_lence nought but feign_ing I
Dein Schwei_gen fass' ich, weichst du mir
cresc.

**Più vivace.**
*Lebhafter.*

deem. Friend - - ship wilt thou still de - ny?
*aus. Wei - - gerst du die Süh - ne mir?*

**Sailors** (without).
***Schiffsvolk** (aussen).*

1st and 2nd Tenor.
1. u. 2. Tenor.

*ff*

Ho! heave ho! heave ho! heave ho! heave — ho! —
*Ho! he! ha! he! ho! he! ha! he! — ha! —*

1st and 2nd Bass.
1. u. 2. Bass.

*ff*

Ho! heave ho, hey!
*Ho! he! ha! he!*

1st and 2nd Bass.
1. u. 2. Bass.

Ho! heave ho, hey!
*Ho! he! ha! he!*

(On an impatient sign from Isolda Brangæna hands her the filled drinking horn.)
*(Auf Isolde's ungeduldigen Wink reicht Brangäne ihr die gefüllte Trinkschale.)*

*ff* *ff* *ff*

**Isolda** (advancing with the cup to Tristan, who gazes fixedly in her eyes).
***Isolde** (mit dem Becher zu Tristan tretend, der ihr starr in die Augen blickt).*

Thou hear'st the cry? The shore's in sight:
*Du hörst den Ruf? Wir sind am Ziel:*

*f*

**rallent.**

(very earnestly)
*(sehr ernst)*

(with slight scorn)
*(mit leisem Hohn)*

we must ere long stand by King Mark to -
*in kur - zer Frist stehn wir vor Kö - nig*

*dimin.* *p* *pp* *p*

Poco steso.
Etwas gedehnt.
geth - er. And wert thou my guide then were it
Mar - ke. Ge - lei - test du mich, dünkt dich's nicht
p
p
well, thus to tell thy tidings: "My lord and
lieb, darfst du so ihm sa - gen: „Mein Herr und
p
king, here is thy queen: 'twere hard to find a fair - er
Ohm, sieh die dir an: ein sanf - t'res Weib gewännst du
poco cresc.
dimin.
bride. Her be - troth - ed hus - band I slaugh - tered, in truth, his
nie. Ih - ren An - ge - lob - ten er - schlug ich ihr einst, sein
p
poco cresc.
head I sent her home; and when I be - neath his
Haupt sandt' ich ihr heim; die Wun - de, die sei - ne
mf
p dolce

weap - ons sank, my hurts were healed by her; when lay my
Wehr mir schuf, die hat sie hold ge - heilt; mein Le - - - ben
dolce
p
p poco cresc.
life with - in her grasp, to me — 'twas grant - ed by — her
lag in ih - rer Macht: das schenk te mir die mil - - de
molto cresc.
f
ff
p
acceler.
grace; she wrought her coun - try sin and shame at a re - quest from
Magd, und ih - res Lan - des Schand' und Schmach, die gab sie mit dar -
acceler.
p
molto cresc.
f
rallent.
a tempo
me thy - mate and queen to be. Such good - ly gifts to fit - ly thank
ein, dein Eh - ge - mahl zu sein. So gu - ter Ga - ben hol - den Dank
rallent.
a tempo
p
with her a kind - ly cup I drank; a crowning act of
schuf mir ein sü - sser Süh - ne - trank; den bot mir ih - re
cresc.

Molto animato.
Sehr bewegt.
grace, my guilt to quite ef - face!"
Huld, zu süh - - nen al - le Schuld!"
SAILORS (without).
SCHIFFSVOLK (aussen).
Tenors.
Tenöre.
Haul the warp!
Auf das Tau!
An - chor down!
An - ker los!
Basses.
Bässe.
cresc.
TRISTAN (starting wildly).
TRISTAN (wild auffahrend).
Down the anchor! Her stern to the stream! The
Los den An-ker! Das Steu - er dem Strom! Den
sails a-weath - er the mast!
Win - - den Se - gel und Mast!
(He takes the cup from her.)
(Er entreisst ihr die Trinkschale.)

I know the queen of Ire-land well, un-questioned are her ma-gic
Wohl kenn' ich Ir-lands Kö-ni-gin und ih-rer Kün-ste Wun-der-
f dim.
p
cresc.
arts:
kraft.
The bal-sam cured me, which she brought; now
Den Bal-sam nützt' ich, den sie bot: den
f
p
cresc.
bid me quaff her cup, that quite I may re-cov-er.
Be-cher nehm' ich nun, dass ganz ich heut' ge-ne-se.
f
ff
f dim.
ff
Heed too my all-a-ton-ing oath, which
Und ach-te auch des Süh-ne-eid's, den
f
in ret-urn I ten-der!
ich zum Dank dir sa-ge!
marc.
p cresc.
ff
ff

(allargando)
(gedehnt)
(vivo)
(rasch)
Tris - tan's honour— high-est truth! Tris - tan's an-guish— brave dis-
Tri - stan's Eh-re— höch-ste Treu'! Tri - stan's E-lend— kühn-ster
(Colla parte.)
(Der Vortrag des Sängers zu beachten!)
meno f
cresc.
(ritenuto)
(zögernd)
(lento)
(langsam)
più p
(appassionato)
(gesteigert)
tress! Trai - tor spi - rit! Dream ill - o - mened! End-less troub-le's
Trotz! Trug des Her - zens! Traum der Ah - nung! Ew'-ger Trau-er
(poco allargando)
(etwas breit)
on - ly truce: o - bli - vion's kind-ly draught,— un -
einz'- ger Trost: Ver - ges - sens güt'-ger Trank,— dich
Molto vivo.
Sehr lebhaft.
(He lifts the cup and drinks.)
(Er setzt an und trinkt.)
ISOLDA.
ISOLDE.
(animato)
(lebhafter)
dread - ed be thou quaff'd! Be-trayed e'en here? I must
trink'— ich son-der Wank! Be - trug auch hier? Mein dic

(She wrests the cup from him.)
(Sie entwindet ihm den Becher.)
halve it!
Hälf - te!
Be - tray - - - -
Ver - rä - - - -
più f
- - er!
- - ther!
I drink to thee!
Ich trink' sie dir!
(She drinks.)
(Sie trinkt.)
molto espr.
ff
Lento.
Langsam.
(Then she throws away the goblet.—Seized with convulsive tremb-
(Dann wirft sie die Schale fort.— Beide, von Schauer erfasst, blicken
dim.
p
più p
trem.
pp
ling they gaze into one another's eyes in the utmost emotion but without stirring, while their expression changes
sich mit höchster Aufregung, jedoch mit starrer Haltung unverwandt in die Augen, in deren Ausdruck der Todestrotz bald
sempre pp
p
from defiance of death to glooming of passion.)
der Liebesgluth weicht.)
(Trembling seizes them. They clutch their hearts tightly
(Zittern ergreift sie. Sie fassen sich krampfhaft an das Herz
Poco mosso.
Etwas bewegt.
pp cresc.
f
ff

and then pass their hands over their brows.
und führen die Hand wieder an die Stirn.
rallent.
Lento.
Langsam.
ff
pp trem.
p
Again their eyes seek to meet,
Dann suchen sie sich wieder mit dem Blick,
are lowered in confusion, and are again turned with rising longing one another.)
senken ihn verwirrt und heften ihn wieder mit steigender Sehnsucht auf einander.)
sehr ausdrucksvoll
p molto espress.
sf
cresc.
più f
ff dim.
ISOLDA (in quivering voice).
ISOLDE (mit bebender Stimme).
Tris - tan!
Tri - stan!
(sinking upon his breast)
(an seine Brust sinkend)
Trai - tor be - lov - ed!
Treu - lo - ser Hol - der!
TRISTAN (with an outburst).
TRISTAN (überströmend).
I - sol - da!
I - sol - de!
(He embraces her passionately.)
(Er umfasst sie mit Gluth.)
Allegro appassionato.
Lebhaft mit Steigerung.
TRISTAN.
TRISTAN.
(They remain in a silent embrace.)
(Sie verbleiben in stummer Umarmung.)
Wo - man di - vine!
Se - lig-ste Frau!
fp

(Brangæna, who confused and trembling, has been leaning over the ship's side with averted face, now turns to observe the love-entranced pair and rushes forwards, wringing her hands in despair.)

*(Brangäne, die mit abgewandtem Gesicht, voll Verwirrung und Schauder sich über den Bord gelehnt hatte, wendet sich jetzt dem Anblick des in Liebesumarmung versunkenen Paares zu und stürzt händeringend voll Verzweiflung in den Vordergrund.)*

BRANGÆNA.
*BRANGÄNE.*

Woe is me!
*We - - - he! Weh!*

1st Tenor.
1. Tenor.
ff
Hail! to King Mark, all hail!
*Heil! Kö - nig Mar - ke Heil!*

ff
Hail! to King Mark, all hail!
*Heil! Kö - nig Mar - ke Heil!*

ff
(Trumpets on the Stage as from the land.)
*(Trompeten auf dem Theater wie vom Lande her.)*

ff f

End - less mis' - ry I have wrought instead of death!
*Un - ab - wend - bar ew' - - - ge Noth für kur - zen Tod!*

f f f f

Dire the deed of my dull, faith - ful
Thör' - - - - ger Treu - - - - - e trug - - vol - les
f
f
f
heart! It cries loud - - - - - - - ly to
Werk blüht nun jam - - - - - mernd em - -
molto cresc.
più f
ff
(Both start from their embrace.)
(Beide fahren aus der Umarmung auf.)
TRISTAN (confused).
TRISTAN (verwirrt).
heav'n!
por!
What troub - - led
Was träum - - te
ff
p dolce
cresc.
dream of Tris - - tan's hon - - - - - our?
mir von Tri - - stan's Eh - - - - - re?
ff
ISOLDA.
ISOLDE.
What troub - led dream of I - sol - - da's
Was träum - te mir von I - sol - - de's
p dolce
cresc.

shame?
Schmach?
Have I re_pulsed thee?
Du mich ver_sto_ssen?
TRISTAN.
TRISTAN.
Have I then lost thee?
Du mir ver_lo_ren?
Frau_dulent
Trü_genden
ff
p
fp
fp
Fren_zy of men_ace, emp_ty threats!
Thö_ri_gen Zür_nens eit_les Dräu'n!
Tris - - tan!
Tri - - stan!
ma_gic, framing de_ceit!
Zau_bers tü_cki_sche List!
I - sol - - - - da!
I - sol - - - - de!
fp
cresc.
ff
Tru - est of men! O how our hearts like o - cean are
Trau - tester Mann! Wie sich die Her - zen wo - gend er_
p
f
p
Sweet - est of maids! O how our hearts like o - cean are
Sü - sse_ste Maid! Wie sich die Her - zen wo - gend er_
ff
p
f
p

cresc.
heav - ing! O how our sen - ses al - most are leav - ing!
he - ben, wie al - le Sin - ne won - nig er - be - ben!
cresc.
heav - ing! O how our sen - ses al - most are leav - ing!
he - ben, wie al - le Sin - ne won - nig er - be - ben!
f
p cresc.
f
p
Lan - guish - ing pas - sion, long - ing and grow - ing,
Seh - nen - der Min - ne schwel - len - des Blü - hen,
p
Lan - guish - ing pas - sion, long - ing and grow - ing,
Seh - nen - der Min - ne schwel - len - des Blü - hen,
p
cresc.
love ev - er yearn - ing, loft - i - est glow - ing!
schmach - ten - der Lie - be se - li - ges Glü - hen!
love ev - er yearn - ing, loft - i - est glow - ing! Rears
schmach - ten - der Lie - be se - li - ges Glü - hen! Jach
f cresc.

Rears in each breast rap - ture con fess'd! Tris -
Jach in der Brust jauch - - zen-de Lust! Tri -
- in each breast rap - - - - ture con-fess'd! I - sol - da!
- in der Brust jauch - - - zen-de Lust! I - sol - de!
più f
f
tan! Tris - tan! World,
stan! Tri - - stan! Wel - - -
I - sol - da! I - sol - - - - - - - -
I - sol - de! I - sol - - - - - - - -
più f
ff
p
Ped.
- I can shun thee, Tris - tan is won me,
- ten ent ron - nen, du mir ge - won - - - nen,
- - - - - - da, I - - sol - - - - - da I have
- - - - - - de, I - - sol - - - - - de mir ge-
Ped.

Tris - tan!
Tri - stan!
Tris - tan is won me, thou'rt my
Du mir ge - won - nen, du mir
won me! I - sol - da!
won - nen! I - sol - de!
Thou'rt my
Du mir
p cresc.
thought all a - bove: high - est de -
ein - zig bewusst, höch - ste
thought all a - bove: high - est de -
ein - zig be - wusst, höch - ste
più f
light of
Lie - bes -
dimin.
f
dimin.
p molto cresc.

(The curtains are pulled wide apart; the whole ship is filled with knights and sailors who joyously hail the shore which is now seen quite near and crowned with a castle on the cliff.)
*(Die Vorhänge werden weit auseinander gerissen; das ganze Schiff ist mit Rittern und Schiffsvolk bedeckt, die jubelnd über Bord winken, dem Ufer zu, das man, mit einer hohen Felsenburg gekrönt, nahe erblickt.)*

love!
*lust!*

BRANGÆNA.
*BRANGÄNE.*
(to the women who at her summons ascend from the cabin)
*(zu den Frauen, die auf ihren Wink aus dem Schiffsraum heraufsteigen)*

(rushing between Tristan and Isolda)
*(zwischen Tristan und Isolde stürzend)*

Quick! the mantle, the roy - al robe!
*Schnell, den Mantel, den Kö - nigsschmuck!*

(Tristan and Isolda remain absorbed in their mutual contemplation, oblivious of what is occurring.)
*(Tristan und Isolde bleiben, in ihren gegenseitigen Anblick verloren, ohne Wahrnehmung des um sie Vorgehenden.)*

love!
*lust!*

più *f*

Poco ritenuto.
*Etwas zurückhaltend.*

BRANGÆNA.
*BRANGÄNE.*

(She puts the royal mantle on Isolda without her noticing it.)
*(Sie legt Isolden, die es nicht gewahrt, den Königsmantel an.)*

Up, hap - less ones! See where are we!
*Un - - sel' - ge! Auf! Hört, wo wir sind!*

*f*

*fortissimo*
*sehr kräftig*

ALL THE MEN (on board ship).
*ALLE MÄNNER (auf dem Schiff).*
Tenors.
Tenöre.

Poco allargando il tempo.
*Etwas breiter im Zeitmass.*

Hail! Hail! Hail! to King Mark, all hail!
*Heil! Heil! Heil! Kö - nig Mar - ke Heil!*

Basses.
Bässe.

più *f*

*ff*

Hail to Mark, the King!
Kö - nig Mar - ke Heil!
Hail!
Heil!
Hail
Heil
f
KURVENAL (entering gaily).
KURWENAL (lebhaft herantretend).
Hail, Tris - tan!
Heil Tri - stan!
our mon - - - - - - - - - arch!
dem Kö - - - - - - - - nig!
cresc.
f
Knight of good hap!
Glück - li - cher Held!
King Mark be - hold ap -
Mit rei - chem Hof - ge -
Hail to our mon - arch!
Heil Kö - nig Mar - ke!
8
f
ff
p

proach - ing in a bark with brave at - ten - dance; glad - ly he stems the
sin - de, dort auf Na - chen naht Herr Mar - ke. Hei! wie die Fahrt ihn
poco cresc.
p
acceler.
tide, coming to seek his bride!
freut, dass er die Braut sich freit!
acceler.
cresc.
KURVENAL.
KURWENAL.
TRISTAN (looking up in bewilderment).
TRISTAN (in Verwirrung aufblickend).
TRISTAN. (Kurvenal poinst over the side.)
TRISTAN. (Kurwenal deutet über Bord.)
Who comes? The King 'tis! What King mean you?
Wer naht? Der Kö - nig! Wel - cher Kö - nig?
ALL THE MEN (waving theier hats).
ALLE MÄNNER (die Hüte schwenkend).
(Tristan gazes senselessly towards the shore.)
(Tristan starrt wie sinnlos nach dem Lande.)
Tenors.
Tenöre.
Hail to King Mark, all hail! Hail to Mark, the King!
Heil! Kö - nig Mar - ke Heil! Kö - nig Mar - ke Heil!
Basses.
Bässe.
ff
ff
Ped.
*

Poco più animato, come prima.
Wieder etwas bewegter.
ISOLDA (bewildered).
ISOLDE (in Verwirrung).
What ist, Bran-gæ-na? What's the cry?
Was ist, Bran-gä-ne? Wel-cher Ruf?
BRANGÆNA.
BRANGÄNE.
I-sol-da! Mis-tress! Compose thy-self!
I-sol-de! Her-rin! Fassung nur heut'!
p
cresc.
ISOLDA.
ISOLDE.
Where am I? liv-ing? What was that draught!
Wo bin ich? Leb' ich? Ha! wel-cher Trank?
BRANGÆNA (despairingly).
BRANGÄNE (verzweiflungsvoll).
The love-po-tion!
Der Lie-bes-trank!
più f
(Isolda stares in terror at Tristan.)
(Isolde starrt entsetzt auf Tristan.)
TRISTAN.
TRISTAN.
ISOLDA.
ISOLDE.
Tris-tan!
Tri-stan!
I-sol-da!
I-sol-de!
ff
ff
(She sinks fainting on his breast.)
(Sie stürzt ohnmächtig an seine Brust.)
Must I live then?
Muss ich le-ben?
BRANGÆNA (to the women).
BRANGÄNE (zu den Frauen).
Look to your la-dy!
Helft der Herrin!
f
più f

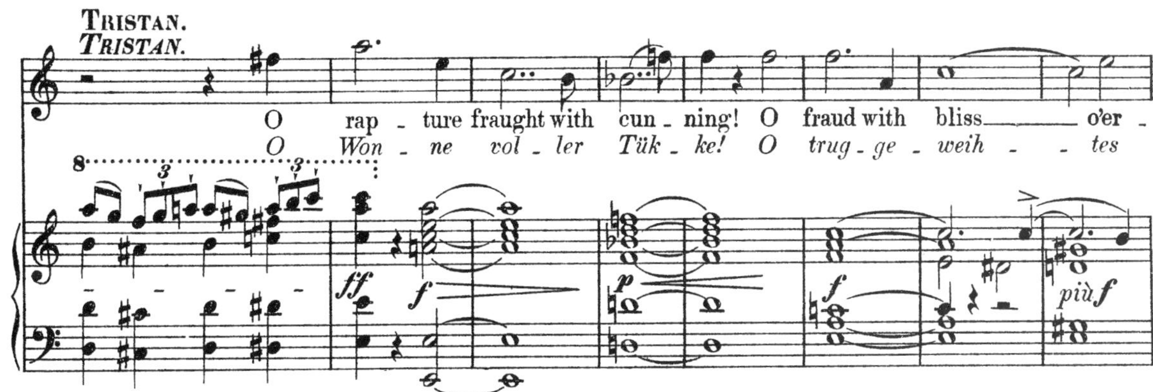

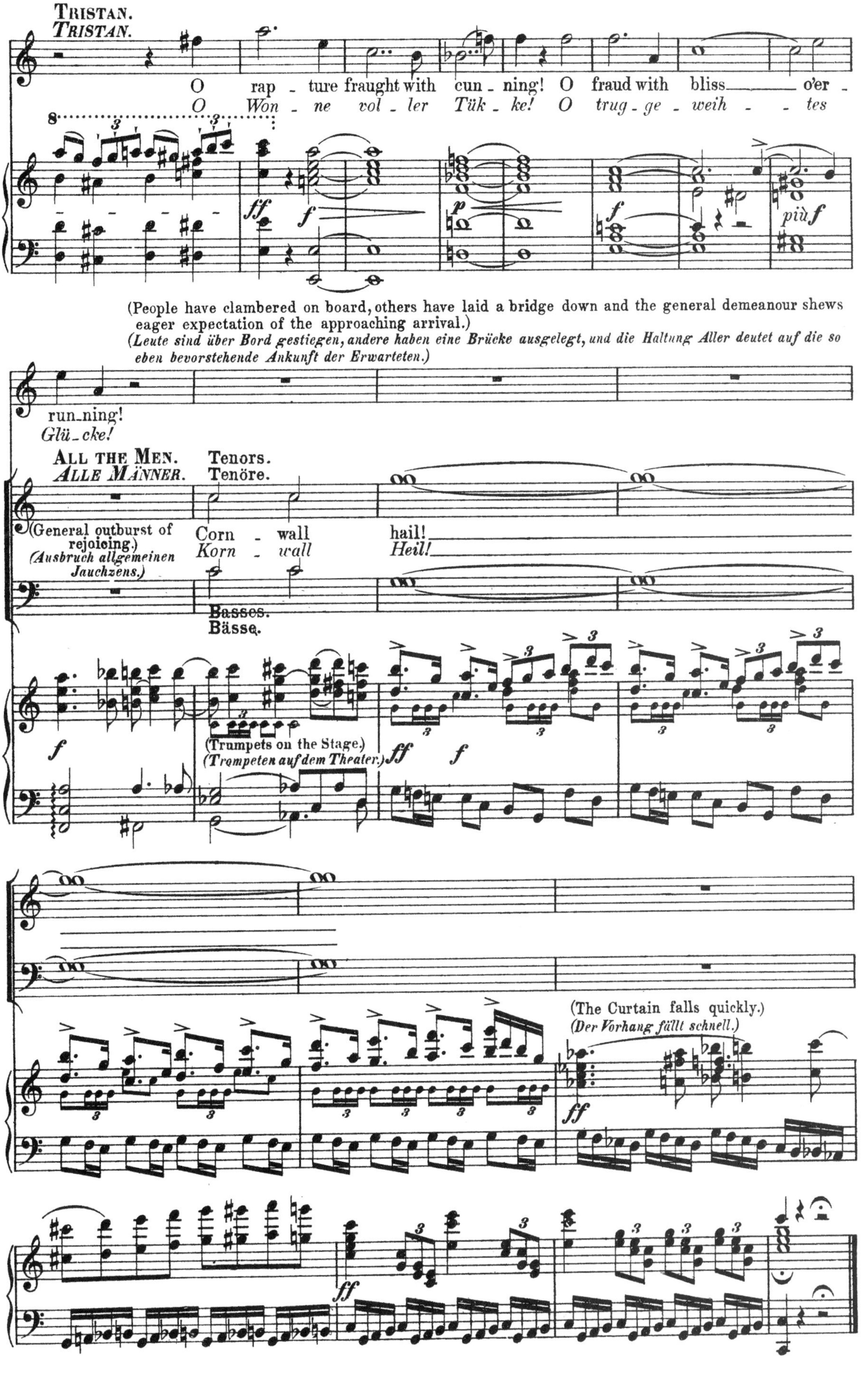

TRISTAN.
TRISTAN.
O rap - ture fraught with cun - ning! O fraud with bliss o'er - running!
O Won - ne vol - ler Tük - ke! O trug - ge - weih - tes Glü - cke!
8
ff
f
p
f
più f
(People have clambered on board, others have laid a bridge down and the general demeanour shews eager expectation of the approaching arrival.)
(Leute sind über Bord gestiegen, andere haben eine Brücke ausgelegt, und die Haltung Aller deutet auf die so eben bevorstehende Ankunft der Erwarteten.)
ALL THE MEN.
ALLE MÄNNER.
(General outburst of rejoicing.)
(Ausbruch allgemeinen Jauchzens.)
Tenors.
Tenöre.
Corn - wall hail!
Korn - wall Heil!
Basses.
Bässe.
f
(Trumpets on the Stage.)
(Trompeten auf dem Theater.)
ff
f
3
(The Curtain falls quickly.)
(Der Vorhang fällt schnell.)
ff
ff

# Second Act.— Zweiter Aufzug.

## Introduction. | Einleitung.

p dolcissimo
sehr zart
pp
molto espressivo
sehr ausdrucksvoll
p
poco a poco cresc.
p
molto cresc.
ff
sempre ff
p

più p
p
poco a poco cresc.
p
molto cresc.
ff
sempre ff
ff
ff
ff
dim.
p
(The Curtain rises.)
(Der Vorhang wird aufgezogen.)

# Scene I. | Erste Scene.

(A garden with high trees before the chamber of Isolda, which lies at one side and is approached by steps. Bright and genial summer night. A burning torch stands at the open door. Sounds of hunting. Brangaena, on the steps, in watching the retreat of the still audible hunt.)

*(Garten mit hohen Bäumen vor dem Gemach Isolde's, zu welchem, seitwärts gelegen, Stufen hinauf führen. Helle, anmuthige Sommernacht. An der geöffneten Thüre ist eine brennende Fackel aufgesteckt. Jagdgetön. Brangäne, auf den Stufen am Gemach, späht dem immer entfernter vernehmbaren Jagdtrosse nach.)*

(Brangaena looks anxiously towards the chamber in which she perceives Isolda approaching.)

*(Brangäne blickt ängstlich in das Gemach zurück, darin sie Isolde nahen sieht.)*

poco cresc.

(Isolda with fiery animation advances from the chamber towards Brangæna.)
*(Isolde tritt, feurig bewegt, aus dem Gemach zu Brangäne.)*

**ISOLDA.**
***ISOLDE.***

Yet do you hear? I — lost the sound some time.
*Hörst du sie noch? Mir — schwand schon fern der Klang.*

*espressivo*
*ausdrucksvoll*

*p* — *più cresc.* — *f* — *più* — *f*

(On the Stage.)
*(Auf dem Theater.)*

*mf*

**BRANGÆNA** (listening).
***BRANGÄNE** (lauschend).*

Still — do they stay: — clear - ly ring the horns.
*Noch — sind sie nah'; — deut - lich tönt's da - her.*

*f* *trem.*

*dim. sempre*

(Isolda listens.)
(Isolde lauscht.)
pp
ISOLDA.
ISOLDE.
Fear but de - ludes thy an - xious ear;
Sor - gen-de Furcht be-irrt dein Ohr;
dolcissimo
sehr zart
più p
sempre pp
immer pp
by sounds of rust - ling leaves thou'rt de -
dich täuscht des Lau - bes säu - selnd Ge -
ceived, a - roused by laugh - ter of
tön, das la - chend schüt - telt der
pp
pp

BRANGÆNA.
BRANGÄNE.
winds. Deceived by wild desire art thou, and but hear'st as would thy will.
Wind. Dich täuscht des Wunsches Ungestüm, zu vernehmen, was du wähnst.
molto cresc.
fp
cresc.
(She listens.)
(Sie lauscht.)
f
trem.
dim.
I still hear the sound of horns.
Ich höre der Hörner Schall.
p
più p
pp
(Isolda listens.)
(Isolde lauscht.)
pp
ISOLDA.
ISOLDE.
No sound of horns were so
Nicht Hörnerschall tönt so

sweet; yon fountain's soft mur - mur_ing cur - rent moves so
hold; des Quel_les sanft rie - seln_de Wel - le rauscht so
qui - - - et - ly hence.
won - - - nig da - her.
If horns yet brayed how could I
Wie hört' ich sie, tos' - ten noch
hear that? In still night a -
Hör - ner? Im Schwei - - - gen der
dolce
zart
pp
lone it laughs on mine ear.
Nacht nur lacht mir der Quell:
My lov'd one hides in
der mei - ner harrt in

dark - - - - - ness un - - seen; wouldst thou
schwei - - - - - gen - der Nacht, als ob
pp
cresc.
hold from my side my dear_est, deem - ing that horns
Hör - - ner noch nah' dir schallten, willst du ihn fern
f dim. p
cresc.
ff
BRANGÆNA.
BRANGÄNE.
thou hear_est? Thy lov'd one
mir hal_ten? Der dei - ner
ff
p
molto cresc.
hid, oh heed my warn - ing! for him do
harrt, o hör' mein War - nen! dess' har_ren
f
f
spies lurk by night. If thou art blinded, are not the eyes of oth_ers
Spä - her zur Nacht. Weil du er_blindet, wähnst du den Blick der Welt er_
p
p
p

burn_ing on thee?
blö_det für euch?
When Tris_tan there on board all trembling
Da dort an Schif_fes Bord, von Tristan's
p
p
brought in his hand the blood_less bride, al_most un_conscious, un_to King Mark, her
be_ben_der Hand, die blei_che Braut, kaum ih_rer mäch_tig, Kö_nig Mar_ke em_
spouse, when all in a_larm turned their eyes on thy face, the kind_ly
pfing, als Al_les ver_wirrt auf die Wan_ken_de sah, der güt'_ge
p
mon_arch, pained and grieved, de_plored that the te_dious voy_age should have
Kö_nig, mild be_sorgt, die Mü_hen der lan_gen Fahrt, die du
p
cresc.
tired thy ten_der frame. But one there was,— I wit_ness'd it well,—
lit_test, laut be_klagt:— ein Einz'_ger war's, ich ach_tet' es wohl,
più f
ff
p
pp

who was watch-ing Tris - tan closely; with e-vil in-tent
der nur Tri-stan fasst' ins Au-ge; mit bös-li-cher List,
told in his eyes, fox-like, his face ob-serving to find out what might
lau-ern-dem Blick sucht' er in sei-ner Mie-ne zu fin-den, was ihm
poco cresc.
poco riten.
a tempo
serve him. List'-ning oft I light up-on him: he lays a se-cret
die-ne. Tü-ckisch lauschend treff' ich ihn oft: der heimlich euch um-
p
cresc.
f
p
snare; of Mel-ot oh be-ware!
garnt, vor Me-lot seid ge-warnt!
f
p
p
ISOLDA.
ISOLDE.
Mean you Sir Mel-ot? O, how you mis-
Meinst du Herrn Me-lot? O, wie du dich
più p
3

take! Is he not Tris - tan's trus - ti - est friend? May my
trügst! Ist er nicht Tri - stan's treu - e - ster Freund? Muss mein
p
pp
true love not meet me, with no one but
Trau - ter mich mei - den, dann weilt er bei
dolce
BRANGÆNA.
BRANGÄNE.
Me - lot he stays. What moves me to fear him makes thee his
Me - lot al - lein. Was mir ihn ver - däch - tig, macht dir ihn
cresc.
friend then! Through Tris - tan to Mark's side is Me - lot's way; he
theu - er! Von Tri - stan zu Mar - ke ist Me - lot's Weg; dort
f
dim.
poco cresc.
sows sus - pi - cion's seed. And those who have to - day on a
sät er üb - le Saat. Die heut' im Rath dies nächt - li - che
più p

night-hunt so sud-den-ly de-cid-ed, a far no-bler game than is guessed by
Ja-gen so ei-lig schnell be-schlossen, ei-nem ed-lern Wild, als dein Wäh-nen
thee tax-es their hunt-er's skill.
meint, gilt ih-re Jä-gers-list.
ISOLDA.
ISOLDE.
For Tris-tan's
Dem Freund zu
dolce
zart
p
sake contrived was this scheme by means of
Lieb' er-fand die-se List aus Mit-leid
Me-lot, in truth. Now would you de-cry his
Me-lot, der Freund. Nun willst du den Treu-en
poco a poco cresc.
friend-ship? He serves I-sol-da bet-ter than you;
schel-ten? Bes-ser als du sorgt er für mich;
cresc.
f

his hand gives help while yours de-nies: What needs the pain of such de-
ihm öff-net er, was mir du sperrst. O spa-re mir des Zö-gerns
cresc.
molto cresc.
più f
lay?— The sig-nal, Brangae-na! O give the
Noth! Das Zei-chen, Brangä-ne! O gieb das
f
p
f
Ped.
sig-nal! Tread out the torch-es tremb-
Zei-chen! Lö-sche des Lich-tes letz-
p
f
p
f
-ling glow, that night may en-
ten Schein! Dass ganz sie sich
p
f
dim.
vel-ope all with her veil! Al-
nei-ge, win-ke der Nacht! Schon
p

read - - - y her peace reigns o'er hill
goss sie ihr Schwei - - - gen durch Hain
and hall, her rap - - - tur - ous
und Haus, schon füllt sie das
awe the heart doth en - thral. Al - low then the
Herz mit won - ni-gem Graus. O lö - sche das
light to fall! Let but the
Licht nun aus, lö - - - - - sche den
dread lus - tre - die! Let
scheu - chen-den Schein! Lass'
più p
pp
poco cresc.
f
più f

BRANGÆNA.
BRANGÄNE.
my be - lov'd draw nigh! The
meinen Lieb - - - - - - - - - sten ein! O
dim.
f
light of warn - ing sup - press not! let it re_mind thee of
lass' die warn _ nen_de Zün _ de! lass' die Ge_fahr sie dir
p
ff
p
per_ il! Ah, woe's me! Woe's me!
zei _ gen! O we - - - - - he! We - - he!
f
più f
Fa - - - - tal fol - ly! The fell pow'r of that po_tion!
Ach mir Ar - men! Des un _ se _ li_gen Trankes!
ff
ff
Poco meno mosso.
Ein wenig mässiger im Zeitmass.
That I framed a fraud for once, thy or_ders to op - pose! Had I been deaf and
Dass ich un_treu ein_mal nur der Her_rin Wil_len trog! Ge_horcht' ich taub und
sf
p
p
p
p

blind, thy work were then thy death: but thy dis-
blind, dein Werk war dann der Tod: doch, dei-ne
cresc.
f
p
cresc.
tress, thy dis-trac-tion of grief, my act
Schmach, dei-ne schmäh-lich-ste Noth, mein Werk
ff
Più animato come prima.
Wieder lebhafter im Zeitmass.
ISOLDA.
ISOLDE.
has con-trived them, I own it! Thy act? O fool-ish
muss ich Schuld'-ge es wissen! Dein Werk? O thör'-ge
p
molto cresc.
f
poco rall.
girl! Love's god-dess dost thou not know? Nor all her
Magd! Frau Min-ne kenn-test du nicht? Nicht ih-res
p cresc.
f
p dolce zart
Poco più moderato ancora.
Ein wenig mässiger als zuvor.
dolce zart
ma-gic gifts? The queen who grants un-
Zau-bers Macht? Des kühn-sten Mu-thes
mf

quail - ing hearts? The witch whose will the world o-beys?
Kö - ni-gin? des Wel - ten-wer-dens Wal - te-rin?
p
f
Life and death she holds in her
Le - - ben und Tod sind un - - ter-than
dolce
zart
pp
p
hands, which of joy and woe
ihr, die sie webt aus Lust
espress.
are wove: she work - eth hate
und Leid, in Lie - - be wan -
in - to love. The work of death I took with-in my own
delnd den Neid. Des To - des Werk, nahm ich's vermes-sen zur
p dolce
fp

hands;
Hand,
Love's god - dess saw and gave her good com - mands.
Frau Min - ne hat es mei - ner Macht ent - wandt.
p
p dolce
accel.
The death condemn'd she claimed as her prey, plan-ning our doom in her own way.
Die Tod-ge-weih-te nahm sie in Pfand, fass-te das Werk in ih-re Hand.
p dol.
f
p
cresc.
Molto ritardando.
Sehr zurückhaltend.
ff
dim.
Moderato con moto.
Mässig bewegt.
How she may bend it, how she may end it, what she may make me, where-so-e'er take me, still
Wie sie es wen - det, wie sie es en - det, was sie mir küh - re, wo-hin mich füh - re, ihr

poco riten.
hers am I sole - ly: so let me o - bey her
ward ich zu ei - gen: nun lass mich ge - hor - sam
cresc.
Più vivace.
Lebhafter bewegt.
Brangæna.
Brangäne.
whol - ly! And if by the art - ful love - potion's
zei - gen! Und muss - te der Min - ne tük - ki-scher
Molto animato.
Sehr bewegt.
lures thy light of rea - son is ravished, if thou art
Trank des Sin - nes Licht dir ver - lö - schen, darfst du nicht
cresc.
reck - less when I would warn thee, this once, oh wait and
se - hen, wenn ich dich war - ne: nur heu - te hör', o
weigh my plead - ing! I im-plore, leave it a - light:
hör' mein Fle - hen! Der Ge-fahr leuch - ten des Licht,

the torch, the torch! O put it not
nur heu - te, heut'! die Fak - kel dort
f dim.
Sempre più mosso.
Immer bewegter. ISOLDA.
ISOLDE.
out this night! She who caus - - - es thus my
lö - sche nicht! Die im Bu - - - sen mir die
p f meno f p cresc.
bo - - - som's throes, whose ea - ger fire with -
Gluth ent - facht, die mir das Her - ze
in me glows, whose light up - on my
bren - - nen macht, die mir als Tag der
f
spi - - - - rit flows, Love's god - - - - - dess
See - - - - le lacht, Frau Min - - - - - ne
sempre
immer f

needs that night should close,
will, es wer - - - de Nacht,
più f
that bright - - - - - - - ly she may
dass hell sie dor - ten
ff
(as she goes quickly towards the torch)
(während sie auf die Fackel zueilt)
reign there and shun the
leuch - te, wo sie dein
dim.
(She takes the torch from the doorway.)
(Sie nimmt die Fackel von der Thür.)
torch - light vain there. Go watch without: keep wa - ry guard! The
Licht ver - scheuchte. Zur War - te du: dort wa - che treu! Die
p
cresc.
sig - - - - - - - - nal, and were it my spi - rit's spark,
Leuch - - - - - - - te, und wär's meines Le - bens Licht,
f
p trem.

smil - - - - - ing,
la - - - - - chend
I'd de-stroy it: hail the
sie zu lö-schen zag' ich
f
p trem.
(She throws the torch to the ground, where it gradually expires.)
(Sie wirft die Fackel zur Erde, wo sie allmählich verlischt.)
dark!
nicht!
ff
ff
(Brangæna, troubled, turns away and ascends by an outer staircase the roof, where she slowly disappears.)
(Brangäne wendet sich bestürzt ab, um auf einer äussern Treppe die Zinne zu ersteigen, wo sie langsam verschwindet.)
f dim.
più p

(Isolda listens and looks, at first timidly towards an avenue.)
(Isolde lauscht und späht, zunächst schüchtern, in einen Baumgang.)
pp
pp
Ped.
più p
pp
Ped.
(Stirred by increasing expectation she goes nearer towards the avenue and looks out more boldly.)
(Von wachsendem Verlangen bewegt, schreitet sie dem Baumgange näher und späht zuversichtlicher.)
p
cresc.
f
p
dolce
(She waves her kerchief at first a little then repeatetly, finally with sorrowful impatience, quicker still.)
(Sie winkt mit einem Tuche, erst seltener, dann häufiger und endlich, in leidenschaftlicher Ungeduld, immer schneller.)
f
cresc.
p
f

p
sempre con Ped.
Sempre più animato.
Immer belebter. (A gesture of sudden transport reveals that she has pereiv-
(Eine Gebärde des plötzlichen Entzückens sagt, dass sie den Freund
ff
p
ed her lover in the distance. She stretches herself higher and higher, to see better over the ground, then hast-
in der Ferne gewahr geworden. Sie streckt sich höher und höher, und, um besser den Raum zu übersehen, eilt sie zur
cresc.
ens back to the steps, from the top of which she beckons to the on-comer.)
Treppe zurück, von deren oberster Stufe sie dem Herannahenden zuwinkt.)
f
più f

## Scene II.— Zweite Scene.

**Tristan and Isolda. | Tristan und Isolde.**

**Molto vivace.**
*Sehr lebhaft.*
(♩ quicker than the previous 𝅗𝅥) (The time here is to keep pace with the expression, now ardent, now tender.)
(♩ *schneller als zuvor* 𝅗𝅥) (*Das Zeitmass ist je nach dem feurigeren oder zärtlicheren Ausdruck gut zu motiviren.*)

ISOLDA.
*ISOLDE.*
Art thou mine? Dare I em-brace thee? At last!
*Bist du mein? Darf ich dich fas-sen? Endlich!*

TRISTAN.
*TRISTAN.*
Do I be-hold thee? Can I be-lieve it?
*Hab' ich dich wie-der? Kann ich mir trau-en?*

(♩ quicker than the previous 𝅗𝅥)
(♩ *schneller als zuvor* 𝅗𝅥)

p cresc.

At last! Do I then clasp thee? *dolce* *zart* Are these thine eyes?
*End-lich! Fühl' ich dich wirk-lich? Dies dei-ne Au-gen?*

Here on my breast! Is it thy own self? *dolce* *zart* These thy
*An meiner Brust! Seh' ich dich sel-ber? Dies dein*

sf p p dolce zart

Here thy-hand? Is't I? Is't thou? held in my arms?
*Hier dei-ne Hand? Bin ich's? Bist du's? Halt' ich dich fest?*

lips? Here thy heart? *p* Is't I? Is't thou?
*Mund? Hier dein Herz? Bin ich's? Bist du's?*

cresc. f p p

molto accel.
accel.
Is it no dream?
Ist es kein Traum?
O
O
Am I not dup_ed?
Ist es kein Trug?
Is it no dream?
Ist es kein Traum?
O
O
molto accel.
accel.
p
molto cresc.
(The 𝅗𝅥 as before in the 2/2.)
(Die 𝅗𝅥 wie zuvor im 2/2.)
rap - ture of spi - rit! O
Won - ne der See - le, o
rap - ture of spi - rit! O
Won - ne der See - le, o
ff
f
sweet_est, high_est, fair_est, strong_est, ho_li_est bliss!
sü_sse, hehr_ste, kühn_ste, schön_ste, se_lig_ste Lust!
sweet_est, high_est, fair_est, strong_est, ho_li_est bliss! End_less plea_sure!
sü_sse, hehr_ste, kühn_ste, schön_ste, se_lig_ste Lust! Oh_ne Glei_che!
p
cresc.

Boundless treasure! Never! Unconceived, ne'er be-
Über-reiche! Ewig! Ungeahnte, nie ge-
Ne'er to sever! Never!
Über-selig! Ewig!
lieved! Joy proclaiming!
kannte! Freudejauchzen!
Overpow'ring exaltation! Bliss outpouring!
Überschwänglich hoch erhab'ne! Lust entzücken!
f
High in heaven, earth ignor-
Himmelhöchstes Welt entrü-
High in heaven, earth ignor-
Himmelhöchstes Welt entrü-
f
più f

ing! Mine!
cken! Mein!
ing! Mine!
cken! Mein!
più f
ff
Tris - tan mine! Tris_tan mine!
Tri - stan mein! Tri_stan mein!
I - sol - da_ mine! I -
I - sol - de_ mein! I -
f
fp
Mine a_lone! Ev - er!
Mein und dein! E - wig!
sol_da mine! Mine a_lone!
sol_de mein! Mein und dein!
fp
fp
più f

Tris - tan mine, I - sol - da ev - er - thine! Tris - tan!
Tri - stan mein, I - sol - de e - wig dein! Tri - stan!
Ev - - - - - - - - - - er! I - sol - da mine! I - sol - da!
E - - - - - - - - - - wig! I - sol - de mein! I - sol - de!
ff
ff
Ped. * Ped. * Ped. * Ped. *
con Ped.
Tris - tan! Ev - - - - - - - - - er, all
Tri - stan! E - - - - - - - - - wig, e - - - - -
I - sol - da! Ev - - - - - - - - - er, all
I - sol - de! E - - - - - - - - - wig, e - - - - -
cresc.
my own!
- - - wig ein!
my own!
- - - wig ein!
ff
ff

How long a - far! How far so long!
Wie lan - ge fern! Wie fern so lang'!
A-part so near! So near yet a -
Wie weit so nah'! So nah' wie
ff
f
dim.
ISOLDA.
ISOLDE.
part! O foe to fond hearts, cru - el far - ness! Wea - ry
weit! O Freun - des-fein - din, bö - se Fer - ne! Trä - ger
f
dim.
f
TRISTAN.
TRISTAN.
time, e - ter - nal-ly lag-ging! O se - par -
Zei - ten zö - gern-de Län - ge! O Weit' und
più f
ff dim.
a - tion! grim ex - ist - ence! Gra - cious near - ness!
Nä - he! hart ent-zwei - te! Hol - de Nä - he!
f
ff
dim.
p

ISOLDE.
ISOLDE.
De - sert dis - - - - - tance! In light I lived, in
Ö - de Wei - - - - - te! Im Dun - kel du, im
cresc.
f
TRISTAN.
TRISTAN.
dark - - - - - - - ness thou! The light! The light!
Lich - - - - - - - te ich! Das Licht! Das Licht!
dim.
p
f
p
O ___ but this light, how long 'twas let to burn! The
O ___ die_ses Licht, wie lang' ver_losch es nicht! Die
dim.
cresc.
sun had sunk, the day had fled; but all their spite not yet was sped: the scar - ing
Son - ne sank, der Tag ver - ging, doch sei_nen Neid er_stickt' er nicht: sein scheuchend
p dolce
sig - nal set they a - light, be - fore my be - lov'd one's dwel - ling, my
Zei - chen zündet er an und steckt's an der Lieb - sten Thü - re, dass

ISOLDA.
*ISOLDE.*

swift approach re - pel - ling. Thy be - lov'd one's hand low - ered the light; for Bran -
*nicht ich zu ihr füh - re. Doch der Lieb - sten Hand lösch - te das Licht; wess' die*

*dim.* *p dolce*

gæ - na's fears in me roused — no fright: while Love's god - dess gave me
*Magd sich wehr - te, scheut' ich — mich nicht: in Frau Min - ne's Macht und*

*espressivo* *ausdrucksvoll* *p* *cresc.* *f* *p* *cresc.*

TRISTAN.
*TRISTAN.*

aid sunlight a mock I made. To sun - - - light!
*Schutz bot ich dem Ta - ge Trutz! Dem Ta - - ge!*

*f* *dim.* *p cresc.* *f*

**Stringendo molto.**
***Heftig drängend im Zeitmass.***

To sun - - - light! To sun - - - light de -
*dem Ta - - - - ge! dem tü - - - - cki - schen*

*più f*

ceiv - ing, our hard - heart - ed foe, give
*Ta - - ge, dem här - - - te - - sten Fein - - - de*

*ff* Ped.

Sempre molto presto.
Immer sehr schnell.
hate and griev - - ing!
Hass und Kla - - ge!
Would I could
Wie du das
dim the bold - vis - aged day as my
Licht, o könnt' ich die Leuch - - - - - te, der
dear one dark - ened her light, our pangs of love to re -
Lie - be Lei - den zu rä - chen, dem fre - chen Ta - ge ver -
quite! Is there a pain, is there a woe it does not wak - en with its
lö - schen! Giebt's ei - ne Noth, giebt's ei - ne Pein, die er nicht weckt mit sei - nem
Molto presto.
Sehr schnell.
Poco ritenuto.
Ein wenig zurückhaltend.
glow? E'en when on all sweet night doth
Schein? Selbst in der Nacht däm - - mern - der
più f
cresc.
dim.

Tempo primo.
Erste Bewegung.
fall, still with thee doth it stay, warn-ing me far a-
Pracht hegt ihn Liebchen am Haus, streckt mir dro-hend ihn
p
p
f
dim.
ISOLDA.
ISOLDE.
way! If still this day-light with me doth stay,
aus! Hegt' ihn die Lieb-ste am eig'-nen Haus,
p dolce
zart
Molto vivace.
Sehr lebhaft.
did not thy heart too hold its ray, when in times gone by my true love,
im eig'-nen Her-zen hell und kraus hegt' ihn trot-zig einst mein Trau-ter,
cresc.
tr
f
f
f
poco riten.
a tempo
Tris-tan, was false to me? Was he not filled with daylight's
Tri-stan, der mich be-trog! War's nicht der Tag, der aus ihm
poco riten.
a tempo
f
p
p espressivo
ausdrucksvoll
f
guile, when he to Ire-land came ere-while, to woo for Mark,
log, als er nach Ir-land wer-bend zog, für Mar-ke mich
p
f
dim.
p cresc.

riten.
a tempo
TRISTAN.
TRISTAN.
the King, and death his dear one to bring? The
zu frei'n, dem Tod die Treu - e zu weih'n? Der
riten.
a tempo
light! The light that round thee shone, and made thee seem a
Tag! Der Tag, der dich um - gliss, da - hin, wo sie der
ve - ry sun! In roy - al radiance thou didst dwell, whom I might ne'er pos-
Son - ne glich, in höch - ster Eh - ren Glanz und Licht, I - sol - den mir ent-
cresc.
sess! So while the sight my eyes did bless, it crushed my heart with
rückt'! Was mir das Au - ge so ent - zückt, mein Her - ze tief zur
p dolce
dim.
sore dis - tress: while day - light thus did shine how
Er - - - de drückt: in lich - ten Ta - ges Schein wie
p cresc.
dim.

Isolda.
Isolde.
could I - sold' be mine? Was she not
war I - sol - de mein? War sie nicht
p
(Il basso molto tenuto.)
(Der Bass möglichst gehalten.)
thine, who chose but thee? What
dein, die dich er - kor? Was
p
cresc.
lies could day-light tell of- me to make thee false-ly sev- - er from one who loved thee
log der bö- se Tag dir- vor, dass, die für dich be-schie - den, die Traute du ver-
f
p
f
dim.
p
Tristan.
Tristan.
ev- er? What shone round thee in
rie- thest? Was dich um - gliss mit
cresc.
f
con molto fuoco
sehr feurig
più f
splen - dour bright, the dazz - ling
hehr - ster- Pracht, der Eh - re
f
più f

charms of pomp and might, of these was I en-amoured, by
Glanz, des Ruh-mes Macht, an sie mein Herz zu han-gen, hielt
ff
dim.
p
wild de-lu-sion glamoured. That which did shed its ra-diant
mich der Wahn ge-fan-gen. Die mit des Schimmers hell-stem
più p
p
cresc.
f
shine a-round this mis-ty brain of mine, the mid-day sun of
Schein mir Haupt und Scheitel licht be-schien, der Wel-ten-Eh-ren
p
cresc.
f
p
f
world-ly glo-ry, with all its
Ta-ges Son-ne, mit ih-rer
p
f
f
accel.
splen-dour's emp-ty sto-ry,
Strah-len eit-ler Won-ne,
accel.
più f

Poco a poco ritardando.
Allmählich zurückhaltend.
trough-out my be-ing seized con - trol to the re - ces - ses
durch Haupt und Schei-tel drang mir ein, bis in des Her - zens
ff dim.
p
più p
of my soul. What there in dark-ness chaste dim-ly obscured I
tief - sten Schrein. Was dort in keu-scher Nacht dun-kel verschlos - sen
p dolce
p dolce
pp
traced, what un-conceived or sought my fan-cies faintly wrought:
wacht, was oh - ne Wiss' und Wahn ich dämmernd dort em - pfah'n:
p dolce
più p
a pic - ture of such beau - ty that eyes re - fused their
ein Bild, das mei-ne Au - gen zu schau'n sich nicht ge -
pp
pp dolce
Poco animando.
Etwas belebend.
du-ty, in the day-light stream - ing o'er me now lay dis-closed be -
trauten, von des Ta - ges Schein be - troffen lag mir's da schimmernd
p poco cresc.

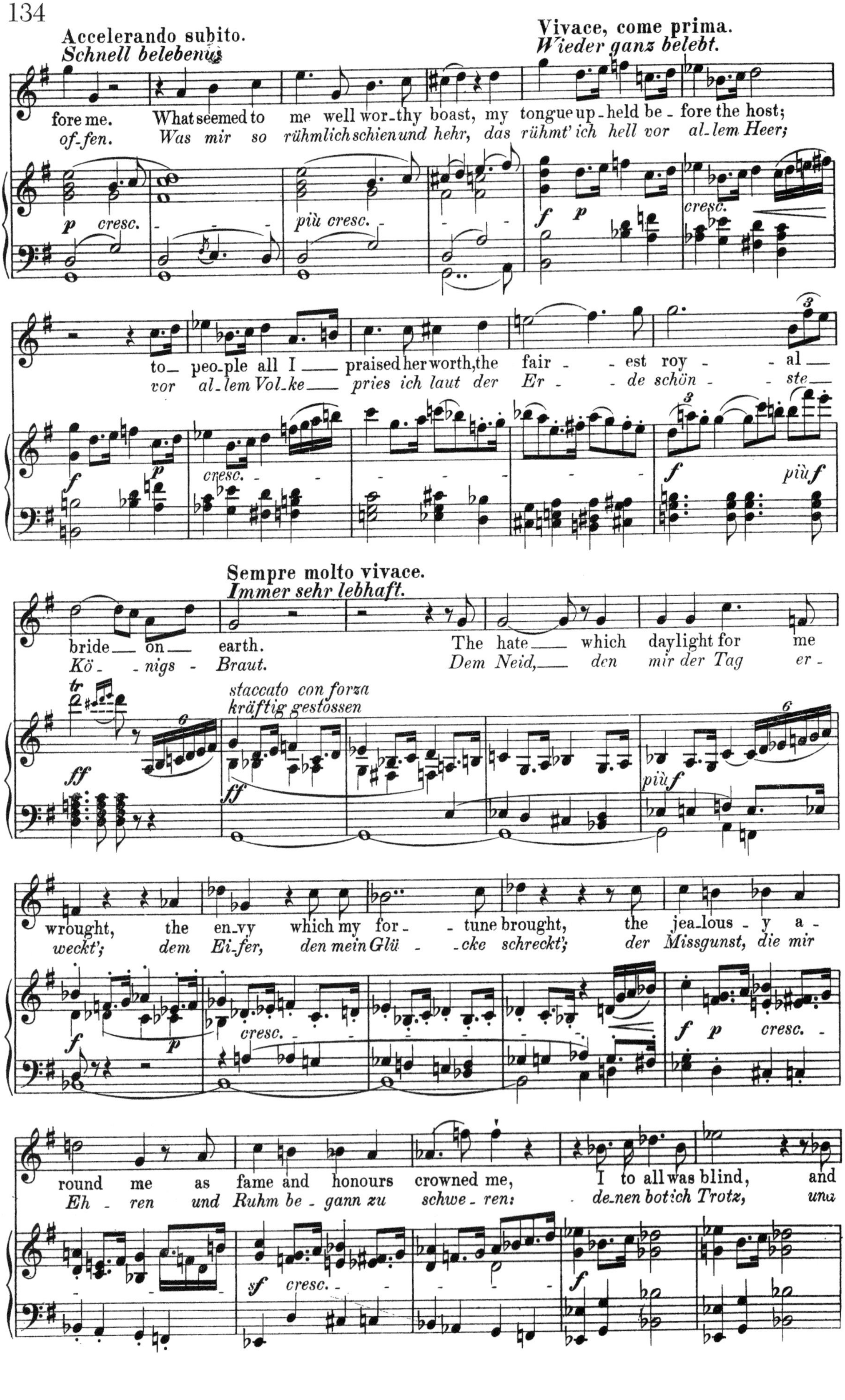

Accelerando subito.
Schnell belebend
Vivace, come prima.
Wieder ganz belebt.
fore me. What seemed to me well wor_thy boast, my tongue up_held be_fore the host;
of_fen. Was mir so rühmlich schien und hehr, das rühmt' ich hell vor al_lem Heer;
p cresc. più cresc. f p cresc.
to_ peo_ple all I praised her worth, the fair - est roy - al
vor al_lem Vol_ke pries ich laut der Er - de schön - ste
f p cresc. f più f
Sempre molto vivace.
Immer sehr lebhaft.
bride on earth. The hate which daylight for me
Kö - nigs - Braut. Dem Neid, den mir der Tag er -
staccato con forza
kräftig gestossen
ff ff più f
wrought, the en_vy which my for - tune brought, the jea_lous - y a -
weckt'; dem Ei_fer, den mein Glü - cke schreckt'; der Missgunst, die mir
f p cresc. f p cresc.
round me as fame and honours crowned me, I to all was blind, and
Eh - ren und Ruhm be_gann zu schwe_ren: de_nen bot ich Trotz, und
sf cresc. f

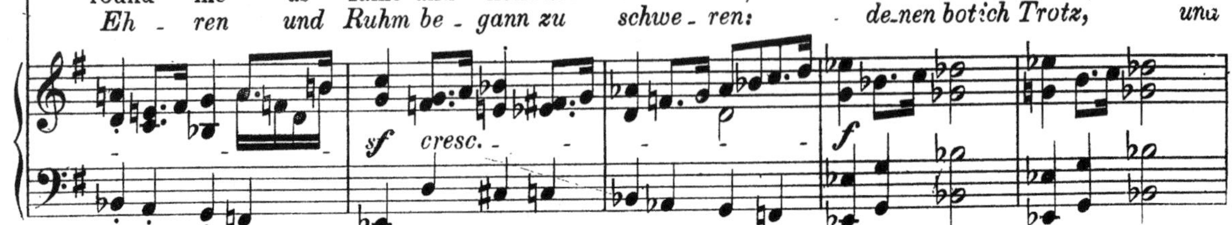

bent my mind to aid my re - pu - ta - tion by seek - ing Ire - land's
treu be - schloss, um Ehr' und Ruhm zu wah - ren, nach Ir - land ich zu
f
f
più f
Allegro molto.
Sehr schnell.
ISOLDA.
ISOLDE.
na - tion. O day - light's slave, in - deed!
fah - ren. O eit - ler Ta - gesknecht!
ff
ff
ff
dim.
p
Sempre molto vivace.
Immer noch sehr bewegt.
De - ceived by that which glam - oured thee, how did I lan - guish while I
Ge - täuscht von ihm, der dich ge - täuscht, wie musst' ich lie - bend um dich
p
molto espressivo
sehr ausdrucksvoll
loved thee! For, to the day - light's ra - diant seem - ing myself in -
lei - den, den, in des Ta - ges fal - schem Pran - gen, von sei - nes
cresc.
f
p

deed a cap-tive deeming, there, — where but love — I'd held a-
Glei-ssens Trug be-fan-gen, dort, — wo ihn Lie- - - be heiss um-
f
espressivo
ausdrucksvoll
p
p
cresc.
bid- - ing, deep in my heart now hate was hid- ing!
fass- - te, im tiefsten Her- - zen hell ich hass- te.
molto cresc.
ff
ff
ff
dim.
Molto vivace.
Sehr lebhaft.
Ah, in my heart's — re-ces- ses, what pangs and wild dis-
Ach, in des Her- - zens Grun- de, wie schmerz- - te tief die
mf
p
sf
molto cresc.
poco riten.
a tempo
p
tress- - ses! How — hard must I have seemed
Wun- - de! Den — dort ich heim- - lich barg,
poco riten.
a tempo
ff
dim.
p dolce
p
cresc.

to him of whom I dreamed, when from the one I che - rished love-
wie dünkt' er mich so arg, wenn in des Ta - ges Schei - ne der
glan - ces waned and pe - rished, as in the day - light's glow he seemed
treu ge - heg - te Ei - ne der Lie - be Bli - cken schwand, als Feind
cresc.
turned to a foe! That which a trai - tor made thee seem, the light of
nur vor mir stand! Das als Ver - rä - ther dich mir wies, dem Licht des
day I sought then to fly: A - way in - to night we two should hie,
Ta - ges wollt' ich ent - flieh'n, dorthin in die Nacht dich mit mir zieh'n,
dim.
Un poco più moderato, ma sempre animato.
Ein wenig mässiger, doch immer noch bewegt.
where I knew de - lu - - - - sion would fade like a
wo der Täu - schung En - - - - de mein Herz mir ver-

dream, where de - ceit ill - o - - - mened would be
hiess, wo des Trug's ge - ahn - - ter Wahn zer -
p
dim.
più p
pp
Poco ritenuto.
Etwas zurückhaltend.
(dolce)
(zart)
end - - ed; there with our hearts for ev - - er blend - ed, in
rin - - ne; dort dir zu trin - ken ew' - ge Min - ne, mit
p
p
Meno ritenuto.
Wieder weniger zurückhaltend.
blest un - ion with me thought I to die with
mir dich im Ver - ein wollt ich dem To - - de
poco cresc.
mf
p dim.
più p
Molto animando.
Sehr belebend.
TRISTAN.
TRISTAN.
thee. The death I prized thy hand did
weih'n. In dei - ner Hand den sü - ssen
p molto cresc.
f
p
lift; when I re - cog-nized the prof - fered gift, when my fore -
Tod, als ich ihn er - kannt, den sie mir bot; als mir die
cresc.

warn - ings ear - nest and true shewed me what deep a - tone - ment was
Ah - nung hehr und ge - wiss zeig - te, was mir die Süh - ne ver-
più cresc.
due,
hiess:
più f
ff
then there gath - ered in mild and ten - der
da er - däm - mer - te mild er - hab' - ner
dim.
p
pp
might with - in my bo - som night: my day was
Macht im Bu - sen mir die Nacht; mein Tag war
cresc.
f dim.
ISOLDA.
ISOLDE.
end - ed quite. But ah! de - ceived thee the faith - less drink; night once a -
da voll - bracht. Doch ach, dich täusch - te der fal - sche Trank, dass dir von
fp
gain from thy grasp did sink: the one who at death's door
Neu - em die Nacht ver - sank: dem ein - zig am To - de
cresc.
p

**Poco rall.** *Etwas zögernd.* **Molto animato.** *Sehr belebt.* **TRISTAN.** *TRISTAN.*

lay, once more a-woke to the day! O
*lag, den gab er wie-der dem Tag! O*

*poco cresc.* *molto cresc.*

hail the po-tion! Hail to the
*Heil dem Tran-ke! Heil sei-nem*

*f* *p* *cresc.* *f*

draught! Hail to its
*Saft! Heil sei-nes*

*p* *molto cresc.* *f* *p* *cresc.*

ma-gic's hap-py craft!
*Zau-bers heh-rer Kraft!*

*f*

Through the door of death
*Durch des To-des Thor,*

*dim.* *p (dolcissimo) (sehr weich)*

*Ped.* *

— to me it flowed; wide and
— wo er mir floss, weit und
p dolce
pp
o - - - - - pen the por - tal showed,
of - - - - - fen er mir er - schloss,
p
where o - ver - come by dreams I had
da - rin ich sonst nur träu - mend ge -
più p
p dolce
stayed, the bliss - - ful realm of
wacht, das Won - ne - reich der
p
p
shade. From the im - age with - in my
Nacht. Von dem Bild in des Her - zens
f
dim.

**Sempre più animando.**
***Immer mehr belebend.***

heart's ——— hidden cell scared was the day - light's du - bi - ous
*ber - - - gendem Schrein scheucht' er des Ta - - ges täu-schenden*

*p dolce* *p*

**accel.**

spell: through night's veil that lay o'er me clear - - - ly it
*Schein, dass nacht - sich - tig mein Au - - ge wahr ——— es zu*

**accel.**

*cresc.*

**Vivace.**
***Lebhaft.***

**ISOLDA.**
***ISOLDE.***

stood ——— be - fore me. But the
*se - - - - hen tau - - - ge. Doch es*

*dim.*

**a tempo**

*f* *p espress.* *cresc.*

*Ped.*

**Più vivace.**
***Immer lebhafter.***

light its fear and de - feat re - paid; with thy mis -
*räch - - te sich der ver - scheuch - - - te Tag; mit dei - nen*

*fp* *f* *p*

deeds a league it made. What thou didst see in
*Sün - den Rath's er pflag: was dir ge - zeigt die*

*f* *p* *fp* *p dolce*

sha - dow - ing night, to the shin - ing sun of
däm - mern - de Nacht, an des Tag - Ge - stir - nes
fp
fp
fp
Molto presto.
Sehr schnell.
king - ly might must thou straight-way sur - ren - der, that
Kö - nigs - macht muss - test du's ü - ber - ge - ben, um
f
p
ff
strascinante
schleppend
it should ex - ist in bright bonds of empty splen -
ein - sam in ö - der Pracht schimmernd dort zu le -
Molto lentando.
Viel langsamer werdend.
p
p
più p
p
Tempo primo. Vivace.
Wieder lebhaftes Zeitmass.
dour. Could I bear it then? Can I bear it still?
ben. Wie er trug ich's nur? Wie er-trag' ich's noch?
Con molto fuoco.
Sehr feurig.
p
più p
p cresc.
molto cresc.
TRISTAN.
TRISTAN.
O now were we to night de -
O, nun wa - ren wir Nacht - ge -
f
ff

vot - - - ed, the dis-honest day with en - vy
weih - - te! Der tü-cki-sche Tag, der Neid - be-
(molto espressivo)
(sehr ausdrucksvoll)
dim.
p
cresc.
f
bloat - ed, ly - ing, could not mis - lead, though it might part us in -
rei - te, tren - nen konnt' uns sein Trug, doch nicht mehr täu - schen sein
p cresc.
f
p
deed! Its pre-ten - tious glow and its gla - mouring
Lug! Sei-ne eit - le Pracht, sei-nen prah - len-den
p
fp
f
light are scout-ed by those who wor - ship night.
Schein ver - lacht, wem die Nacht den Blick ge - weiht:
f
dim.
p
All its fli-ckering gleams in flashes out - blazing blind our eyes no
sei-nes flackernden Lich - tes flüch-ti-ge Blit-ze blen - den uns nicht
cresc.
p

more. Those who death's dark night bold-ly sur-vey,
mehr. Wer des To-des Nacht lie-bend er-schaut,
più p
p espress.
those who have stud-ied her se-cret way, the day-light's false-hoods,
wem sie ihr tief Ge-heim-nis ver-traut: des Ta-ges Lü-gen,
più p
sf
accel.
rank and fame, ho-nour and all at which men aim, to them are no more
Ruhm und Ehr', Macht und Ge-winn, so schim-mernd hehr, wie eit-ler Staub der
sf
cresc.
fp
mat-ter than dust which sun-beams scatter!
Son-nen sind sie vor dem zer-sponnen!
f dim.
In the day-light's vi-sions
In des Ta-ges eit-lem
pp
cresc.

accel.
throng - ing on - ly a - bides one long -
Wäh - nen bleibt ihm ein ein - zig Seh -
molto cresc.
Poco steso.
Etwas gedehnt.
ing; we yearn to hie to ho - ly night, where un - end - ing,
nen, das Seh - nen hin zur heil' - gen Nacht, wo ur - e - wig,
ff
ff
Rallentando sempre poco a poco.
Langsamer, und allmählich immer langsamer.
on - ly true, Love ex - tend - eth de - light.
ein - zig wahr, Lie - bes - won - ne ihm lacht.
dim.
più p
tr
(Tristan draws Isolda gently down to a flowery bank at one side, sinks on his knees before her and rests his head
(Tristan zieht Isolde sanft zur Seite auf eine Blumenbank nieder, senkt sich vor ihr auf die Knie und schmiegt sein Haupt
p dolce
on her arm.)
in ihren Arm.)
più p
pp
r. H.
sf

più p
dim.
pp dolce
Lento moderato.
Mässig langsam.
pp
ISOLDA.
ISOLDE.
O
O
TRISTAN.
TRISTAN.
O night of rap - ture rest up -
O sink' her - nie - - der, Nacht der
pp
night of rap - ture rest up - on us!
sink' her-nie - - der, Nacht der Lie - - - be,
on us! lift our lives' re-mem - brance
Lie - - - be, gieb Ver-ges - - sen, dass ich
poco cresc.

lift — our lives' — re-mem-brance from us,
gieb — Ver-ges - sen, dass ich le - - - - be,
from us,
le - - - be,
let — us but — a-bide — with
nimm — mich auf — in dei - nen
dim.
let — us but — a-bide with thee;
nimm mich auf — in dei-nen Schoss,
thee;
Schoss,
p
from the world, oh set us
lö - se von der Welt mich
from the world, oh set us free!
lö - se von der Welt mich los!
più p
pp
Tristan.
free!
los!
Ex - tin - guished in the twi - - light's stream - ing
Ver - lo - schen nun die letz - - te Leuch - te;
(dolce)
pp (zart)
Isolde.
all our doubt - ing, all our dream - ing,
was wir dach - ten, was uns däuch - te;
(dolce)
p (zart)
più p

ISOLDA.
ISOLDE.
all our fan - cies,
all' Ge - mah - nen,
TRISTAN.
TRISTAN.
all our mem' - ries,
all' Ge - den - ken,
p espress.
poco cresc.
sa - cred twi - light's soft ad -
heil' - ger Dämm' - rung heh - res
sa - cred twi - light's soft ad - van - ces
heil' - ger Dämm' - rung heh - res Ah - nen
p
poco cresc.
poco f
p
van - ces bid vain fears to cease,
Ah - nen löscht des Wäh - nens Graus
bid vain fears to cease, from
löscht des Wäh - nens Graus welt -
cresc.
molto cresc.

Allargando.
Breiter.
Ritenuto e largo.
Sehr breit und zurückhaltend.
riten.
from the world re - lease.
welt - - - - - er - lö - - - - send aus.
the world re - lease.
- - er - lö - - send aus.
ff
dim.
p
Isolda.
Isolde.
Lento moderato, come prima.
Wieder mässig langsam.
p tranquillo
ruhig
Hid our hearts a - way sunlight's stream - ing, bliss would bloom
Barg im Bu - sen uns sich die Son - ne, leuch - ten la -
Molto tranquillo.
Sehr ruhig.
from stars' tender beam - ing.
chend Ster - ne der Won - ne.
Tristan.
Tristan.
To thy en - chant - ment we sur - ren - der be -
Von dei - nem Zau - ber sanft um - spon - nen, vor
sempre
immer p
neath thy gaze so won - drous ten - der.
dei - nen Au - gen süss zer - ron - nen,
Isolda.
Isolde.
Heart to heart, and lip to
Herz an Herz dir, Mund an
p dolce

lip.
Mund;
Bliss - ful beams our eyes are
bricht mein Blick sich wonn' - er -
TRISTAN.
TRISTAN.
Each the oth - er's breath we sip.
ei - nes A - thems ein' - ger Bund;
Bliss - ful beams
bricht mein Blick
p dolce
p dolce
bind - ing, a - bashed is earth with ra - diance blind - ing:
blin - det, er - bleicht die Welt mit ih - rem Blen - den:
più p
our eyes are bind - ing, a - bashed is earth with ra - diance
sich wonn' - er - blin - det, er - bleicht die Welt mit ih - rem
più p
pp
lit by the day - light's dazz - ling lie,
die uns der Tag trü - gend er - hellt,
blin - ding:
Blen - den:
un - daunt - ed by falsehoods which we de -
zu täu - schendem Wahn ent - ge - gen - ge -
p
p
p
cresc.

accel.
thou'rt my world, thine am I
selbst dann bin ich die Welt:
fy, thou'rt my world, thine am I
stellt, selbst dann bin ich die Welt:
accel.
ff
Ped. * Ped. * Ped. * Ped. *
Tempo primo.
Erstes Tempo.
Won - drous rap - ture
Won - ne - hehr - stes
Won - drous rap - ture
Won - ne - hehr - stes
Tempo primo.
Erstes Tempo.
dim.
6 6
Ped. *
p
weav - ing,
We - ben,
p
weav - ing,
We - ben,
3
molto cresc.
p
Ped. *

f
rallent.
che - rish'd vi - sions a - chiev - ing,
Lie - be - hei - lig - stes Le - ben,
dim.
f
dim.
che - rish'd vi - sions a - chiev - ing,
Lie - be - hei - lig - stes Le - ben,
rallent.
ff (molto espress.)
(sehr ausdrucksvoll)
dim.
p
più p
a tempo
p
ne'er daunt - ed by day - light's beam be
Nie - wie - der - er - wa - chens wahn - los
p
ne'er daunt - ed by day - light's beam be
Nie - wie - der - er - wa - chens wahn - los
a tempo
pp
più p
morendo
ersterbend
our un - dy - ing dream.
hold be - wuss - ter Wunsch.
morendo
ersterbend
our un - dy - ing dream.
hold be - wuss - ter Wunsch.
(Tristan and Isolda sink down on the flowery bank completely carried away by passion and remain reclining thus with heads in contact.)
(Tristan und Isolde versinken in gänzliche Entrücktheit, in der sie, Haupt an Haupt auf die Blumenbank zurückgelehnt, verweilen.)
pp
6

BRANGÆNA (from the turret, invisible).
BRANGÄNE (von der Zinne her, unsichtbar).
p
Long I watch a-
Ein - sam wa - chend
lone by night:
in der Nacht,
poco cresc.
ye en - wrapt in love's
wem der Traum der Lie -
dim.
più p
de - light,
be lacht,
p espressivo
ausdrucksvoll
dim.
(appassionato)
(gesteigert)
heed my bod -
hab' der Ei
p
dim.
p espressivo
ausdrucksvoll

- - ing voice a - - - -
- - nen Ruf in
dim.
p
dim.
right. I fore - warn you
Acht, die den Schlä - - - fern
dolcissimo e molto espressivo
sehr zart und ausdrucksvoll
p
p
woe is near: wak - - - - - - -
Schlim - - mes ahnt, ban - - - - - - -
dim.
p
- - - - en to my words
- - - - ge zum Er - wa - - - - - -
p
dim.
p
Molto tranquillo.
Sehr ruhig.
- of fear!
- - chen mahnt!
dolce

Have a care!
Ha - bet Acht!
Have a care!
Ha - bet Acht!
Swift - ly night doth wear!
Bald ent - weicht die Nacht!
morendo
verhallend
morendo
morendo
Sempre molto tranquillo.
Immer sehr ruhig.
ISOLDA.
ISOLDE.
List, be - lov - ed!
Lausch', Ge - lieb - ter!
cresc.
dim.

TRISTAN.
TRISTAN.
Let me_ die thus!
Lass mich ster_ben!
ISOLDA (gradually raising herself a little).
ISOLDE (allmählich sich ein wenig erhebend).
En - - vious
Neid' - - sche
molto espressivo
sehr ausdrucksvoll
p
TRISTAN (remaining reclining).
TRISTAN (zurückgelehnt bleibend).
watcher! I'll ne'er wak_en!
Wache! Nie er - wa_chen!
ISOLDA.
ISOLDE.
But the day___ must dawn and rouse thee?
Doch der Tag___ muss Tri - stan wek_ken?
f
dim.
più p
TRISTAN (raising his head a little).
TRISTAN (ein wenig das Haupt erhebend).
Let the Day to_ Death sur - ren - - der!
Lass den Tag dem To - - de wei - - chen!
Poco animando.
Ein wenig belebend.
cresc.
dim.
p
ISOLDA (senz' impeto).
ISOLDE (nicht heftig).
Day___ and Death___ will both en - gen - - der feud a - gainst_ our pas - -
Tag___ und Tod___ mit glei_chen Strei - - chen soll - ten uns - re Lieb'___
p
p
p
p

Molto tranquillo.
Sehr ruhig.
TRISTAN (raising himself slightly).
TRISTAN (sich mehr aufrichtend).
-sion ten - der. Aye, our pas-sion! Thine and mine love!
- er-rei - chen? Uns - re Lie-be? Tris - tan's Lie - be?
cresc.
p dolce
Tris-tan and I-sol - da's pas - sion! How could Death al-
Dein' und mein', I-sol - de's Lie - be? Wel - ches To - des
p
cresc.
f
loy it, weak-en or des-troy it!
Strei - chen könn-te je sie wei - chen?
p
cresc.
f dim.
più f
molto tranquillo
sehr ruhig
Came he to me, this might-y Death threat'ning to end for ev-er my breath which I would
Stünd' er vor mir, der mächt'ge Tod, wie er mir Leib und Le-ben be-droht, die ich so
pp
p
p
p
più p

poco ritenuto
a tempo
etwas zurückhaltend
gladly for love relinquish if e'en his stroke descended, would Love itself then be ended?
willig der Liebe lasse, wie wäre seinen Streichen die Liebe selbst zu erreichen?
poco ritenuto
a tempo
pp
cresc.
Poco ritenuto e molto tranquillo.
Etwas zögernd und sehr ruhig.
(nestling with his head yet closer to Isolda)
(immer inniger mit dem Haupte sich an Isolde schmiegend)
f
dim.
più p
Died I for that which I fain would die for, how could that Love with me be ended? The pow'r immortal with me to perish?
Stürb' ich nun ihr, der so gern ich sterbe, wie könnte die Liebe mit mir sterben, die ewig lebende mit mir enden?
pp
poco cresc.
più cresc.
molto espressivo
sehr ausdrucksvoll
f
ff
If
Doch,
Lento (come prima).
Langsam (wie zuvor).
tempo
Love can ne'er die in Tristan, how then can Tristan die in
stürbe nie seine Liebe, wie stürbe dann Tristan seiner
p
cresc.
ff
dim.
p
ff

Poco rallent.
Etwas zögernd.
lov - - - - - - - ing?
Lie - - - - - - - be?
dim.
più p
pp
Animando, ma molto poco.
Etwas belebend, aber unmerklich.
ISOLDA.
ISOLDE.
p
But __ our af - fec - - tion,
Doch __ uns - re __ Lie - - be,
dolcissimo
sehr weich
p espress.
is it not Tris - - tan's and __ I - sol - da's? That
heisst sie nicht Tris - - tan und __ I - sol - de? Dies
poco riten.
a tempo
più p
p
espressivo
ausdrucksvoll
word __ of sweetness, "and": __ Love it bind - eth
sü - - sse Wört-lein: und, __ was es bin - det,
più p
pp dolce
in ten - der band, __ if __ Tristan died __ would Death not loos - en
der Lie - be Bund, __ wenn Tristan stürb', __ zer - stört' es nicht der
poco cresc.

Molto tranquillo.
Sehr ruhig.
TRISTAN (molto tranquillo).
TRISTAN (sehr ruhig).
this? Though came to us Death, what could he kill but all that
Tod? Was stür-be dem Tod, als was uns stört, was Tri-stan
pp
con Ped.
ill which for-ces our lives to sev-er, hin-dering our love for
wehrt, I-sol-de im-mer zu lie-ben, e-wig ihr nur zu
più p
ISOLDA.
ISOLDE.
ev-er? That little word, though, "and": were it destroyed, un-
le-ben? Doch dieses Wört-lein: und, wär' es zerstört, wie
pp
cresc.
sf
lento
langsam
less the life of I-sold' were like-wise riv-en, could Tris-tan to death be
an-ders als mit I-sol-de's eig'nem Le-ben wär' Tris-tan der Tod ge-
p
cresc.
ff dim.
Con moto.
Nicht schleppend.
(Tristan, with expressive gestures, draws Isolda gently to him.)
(Tristan zieht, mit bedeutungsvoller Gebärde, Isolde sanft an sich.)
TRISTAN.
TRISTAN.
giv-en? O
ge-ben? So
p dolce
più p
pp
ppp

The six quavers exactly equivalent to those of the late 3/4 movement.
Die sechs ♪ genau den sechs ♪ des frühern 3/4 Takts entsprechend.
might we then to - - - geth - er die, each the oth - er's
star - ben wir, um un - - ge - trennt, e - wig ei - nig,
pp trem.
pp
own for aye, nev - er fear - ing, nev - er wak - ing,
oh - ne End', ohn' Er - wa - chen, ohn' Er - ban - gen,
sempre
immer pp
(accrescendo)
(gesteigert)
dim.
blest de - lights of love par - tak - ing, each to each be
na - men - los in Lieb' um - fan - gen, ganz uns selbst ge -
p
più p
(ISOLDA looking up at him in thoughtful absorption.)
(ISOLDE wie in sinnender Entrücktheit zu ihm aufblickend.)
p
O might we then to - geth - er
So stürben wir, um un - ge -
dim.
giv - en, in love a - lone our heav - en!
ge - ben, der Lie - be nur zu le - - ben!
morendo poco cresc. mf dim.
più p
pp
pp

die,—
trennt,—
never fearing,
ohn' Erwachen,
each the other's own for aye,—
ewig einig, ohne End',
sempre
immer
pp
nev - er waking,—
ohn' Er - bangen,—
blest — delights of
na - - menlos in
of
in
poco cresc.
love — partaking each to each be giv -
Lieb' — umfangen, ganz uns selbst gege -
love — partaking each to each be giv -
Lieb' — umfangen, ganz uns gege -
pp
cresc.

en, in love a - lone our heav - - - -
ben, der Lie - be nur zu le - - - -
en, in love a - lone our heav - - - -
ben, der Lie - be nur zu le - - - -
p
dolce
dim.
più p
(Isolda, as if overpowered, droops her head upon his breast.)
(Isolde neigt, wie überwältigt, das Haupt an seine Brust.)
- - - en!
- - - ben!
BRANGÆNA (as before).
BRANGÄNE (wie vorher).
f
Have a care!
Ha - bet Acht!
- - - en!
- - - ben!
pp
un poco cresc.
BRANGÆNA.
BRANGÄNE.
f
Have a care! Night
Ha - bet Acht! Schon
dim.
yields to day - - - - light's glare!
weicht dem Tag die Nacht!
morendo
verhallend
morendo
morendo

TRISTAN (bends smilingly down to Isolda).
TRISTAN (lächelnd zu Isolde geneigt).
(Isolda gazes fondly up at Tristan.)
(Isolde, schwärmerisch zu Tristan aufblickend.)
Shall I lis - - - ten?
Soll ich lau - - - schen?
pp
f dim.
ISOLDA.
ISOLDE.
riten. a tempo
Let me die thus!
Lass mich ster-ben!
TRISTAN (more gravely).
TRISTAN (ernster).
Must I wak - en?
Muss ich wa - chen?
riten. a tempo
p
ISOLDA (more affected).
ISOLDE (bewegter).
riten. a tempo
Nought shall wake me!
Nie er - wa-chen!
TRISTAN (stringendo).
TRISTAN (drängender).
Must not day - light dawn and
Soll der Tag noch Tri - stan
riten.
a tempo
un poco più stringendo
etwas drängender
f dim.
p
p
rouse me?
we - cken?
cresc.
ISOLDA (with enthusiasm).
ISOLDE (begeistert).
Let the Day to Death sur -
Lass den Tag dem To - de
molto riten.
f molto espressivo
sehr ausdrucksvoll
molto riten.
p

Sempre più animando.
Immer mehr belebend.
TRISTAN.
TRISTAN.
ren-der! May thus the day's e - vil threats be de - -
wei-chen! Des Ta - ges Dräu - en nun trotz - - ten wir
cresc.
f
ISOLDA (with rising extasy).
ISOLDE (mit wachsender Begeisterung).
fied? From its thral - - - - - - dom let us
so? Sei - nem Trug e - - - wig zu
f
dim.
Sempre più mosso.
Immer belebter.
TRISTAN.
TRISTAN.
fly! And shall not its dawn be dread - ed by
flieh'n! Sein däm - mern-der Schein ver - scheuch - te uns
p
cresc.
Allegro, con elevazione.
Lebhaft, mit Steigerung.
ISOLDA (with ecstatic gesture, rising to her feet).
ISOLDE (mit grosser Gebärde ganz sich erhebend).
(Tristan follows her, they embrace in
(Tristan folgt ihr, sie umfangen sich in
Night will shield us for aye!
E - - - wig währ' uns die Nacht!
us?
nie?
f
p
cresc.
fp
fp

a fond ecstasy.)
schwärmerischer Begeisterung.)
fp
fp
fp molto cresc.
rallent.
Molto vivo e presto.
Sehr lebhaft und schnell.
O end - less night,
O ew' - ge Nacht,
O end - less night,
rallent.
O ew' - ge Nacht,
più f
ff
dim.
bliss - ful night!
sü - sse Nacht!
bliss - ful night!
sü - sse Nacht!
p dolce
p
molto cresc.
Glad and glo - rious lov -
Hehr er - hab' - ne Lie -
Glad and glo - rious lov -
Hehr er - hab' - ne Lie -
ff
dim.
p dolce

- - ers' night! Those whom thou hold - - est,
- - bes nacht! Wen du um - fan - - gen,
- - ers' night! lapp'd in de -
- - bes - nacht! wem du ge -
p
più p
pp
how could e'en the bold - - - est un - - moved en -
wie wär' oh - ne Ban - - - gen aus dir er
light, how could e en the bold - est
lacht, wie wär' oh - ne Ban - gen
p
cresc.
dure thy flight? Now end all our an - guish,
je - er - wacht? Nun ban - ne das Ban - gen,
dim.
e'er endure thy flight? Now end all our
er aus dir er - wacht? Nun ban - - - ne das
f
dim.
p

gra - cious Death, see how we lan - guish,
hol - der Tod, seh - - - - nend ver - lang - ter
an - guish, see how we lan - guish,
Ban - gen, seh - - - - nend ver - lang - ter
cresc.
ff
dim.
dim.
lov - ing Death! In thine arms tak - en, thou our
Lie - bes - tod! In dei - nen Ar - men, dir ge
p
dim.
lov - ing Death! In thine arms
Lie - bes - tod! In dei - nen
p
più p
dolce
friend, we fear not to wak -
weiht, ur - - - hei - lig Er - war -
tak - en, thou our friend, we
Ar - men, dir ge - weiht, ur
poco cresc.
più cresc.

ff
en from the trans - port thou dost lend.
men, von Er - wa - chen's Noth be - freit!
fear not to wak - en from the transport thou dost lend.
hei - lig Er - war - men, von Er - wa - chen's Noth be - freit!
molto cresc.
ff
f dim.
p
How to take it, how to break it,
Wie es fas - sen, wie sie las - sen,
p espress.
p
Sun - light dis - tant
Fern der Son - ne,
f
p
joy ex - ist - ent, sun - light dis - tant,
die - se Won - ne, fern der Son - ne,
cresc.
p

far from mourn - ing, sor - row - warn - ing!
fern der Ta - - ge Tren - nungs - kla - - ge!
far from mourn - - - - - - ing, sor - - row-
fern der Ta - - - - - - ge Tren - - nungs-
f
dim.
p
Fan - cies spurn - ing,
Oh - ne Wäh - nen
dolce
zart
warn - ing! soft - - ly yearn - - ing;
kla - ge! sanf - - tes Seh - - nen;
dolce
p
fears ex - pir - ing,
oh - - ne Ban - gen
p
sweet de - sir - - ing;
süss Ver - lan - - gen;
dolce
p
p

glad - ly - dy - ing;
hehr Ver - ge - hen;
p
an - guish fly - ing, glad - ly dy - ing;
oh - ne We - hen hehr Ver - ge - hen;
dolce
p
p
p
no more pin - ing, night - en - shrin - ing;
oh - ne Schmach - ten hold Um - nach - ten;
p
night - en - shrin - ing;
hold Um - nach - ten;
dolce
p
p
what be -
oh - ne
cresc.
ne'er di - vid - ed, what be - tid - ed,
oh - ne Mei - den, oh - ne Schei - den,
p
molto cresc.

tid - - - - - - ed, side by side
Schei - - - - - - den, traut al - lein,
side by side
traut al - - - - lein,
f
più f
pp
e'er a - - bide in realms of space un -
e - - wig heim, in un - ge - - mess' - - nen
e'er a - bide in realms of space un -
e - - - - wig heim, in un - - ge - mess' - - nen
poco cresc.
p
mea - sured, vi - - - - - - - sion blest and
Räu - men ü - - - - - - ber - sel' ges
mea - - - - - sured, vi - - - - - - sion
Räu - - - - - - men ü - - - - - - ber -
dim.
più p
pp
Ped.
Ped.

trea - sured: Thou I - sol - da,
Träu - men: Du I - sol - de,
dolce
zart
blest and trea - sured: Tris - tan
sel' - ges Träu - men: Tris - tan
dolce
Tris - tan I,
Tris - tan ich,
thou,
du,
I I -
ich, I -
p dolce
no more I - sol - da!
nicht mehr I - sol - de!
sol - da,
sol - de,
no more
nicht mehr
più p
pp

Molto affrettando.
Sehr drängend.
Never spoken, never broken,
Ohne Nennen, ohne Trennen,
Tristan! Endless!
Tristan! Ewig!
morendo
p molto cresc.
newly sighted, newly lighted, endless
neu Erkennen, neu Entbrennen, endlos
Ever! Endless
Endlos! End
f
ever all our dream:
ewig ein bewusst:
less ever all our dream, ever
los ewig ein bewusst, ewig
più f
ff molto tenuto ma non legato
sehr gehalten, aber nicht gebunden
ff

Sempre poco stringendo.
Immer etwas drängend.
end - - - - less
end - - - - los
ev - er
e - wig
all our dream: ev - er end - less
ein - be - wusst: e - wig end - los
sempre
immer f
in our bo - som's gleam
heiss er - glüh - ter Brust
love - de -
höch - - ste
mp
end - less ev - - er
end - los e - - wig
lights su - preme!
Lie - bes lust!
in our
Heiss er - -
più f

Più stringendo.
Noch drängender.
love - de-
höch - - - - - - ste
bo - - - - som's gleam love - de - lights
glüh - - - - ter Brust höch - ste Lie - - -
legato
gebunden
p
cresc.
lights su - preme! Love -
Lie - - - bes - lust! Höch - - - - - -
su - preme! Love - de - lights su - preme!
- - - bes - lust! Höch - ste Lie - bes - lust!
non legato
nicht gebunden
molto cresc.
de - lights su -
ste Lie - - - - bes -
Love - de - lights su -
Höch - - - ste Lie - - - - bes -
più f

# Scene III. | Dritte Scene.

**Prestissimo.(𝅗𝅥 perceptibly quicker than before.)**
*Sehr schnell.(𝅗𝅥 merklich schneller als zuvor.)*

**ISOLDA.**
***ISOLDE.***

preme!
*lust!*

**BRANGÆNA** (utters a piercing shriek).
***BRANGÄNE*** *(stösst einen grellen Schrei aus).*

(Schriek.)
*(Schrei.)*

**TRISTAN** (Tristan and Isolda remain in their enraptured state).
***TRISTAN*** *(Tristan und Isolde bleiben in verzückter Stellung).*

preme!
*lust!*

**KURVENAL** (rushing in with drawn sword).
***KURWENAL*** *(stürzt mit entblösstem Schwert herein).*

Save yourself,
*Ret - te dich,*

ff
fp molto cresc.

(He looks off behind him in great alarm.)
*(Er blickt mit Entsetzen hinter sich in die Scene zurück.)*

Tristan!
*Tristan!*

f
ff

(Mark, Melot and courtiers (in hunting array) come from the avenue quickly towards the front, and pause in amaze-
*(Marke, Melot und Hofleute (in Jägertracht) kommen aus dem Baumgange lebhaft nach dem Vordergrunde und halten ent-*

**The previous tempo. (𝅗𝅥 slower.)**
***Wieder das vorhergehende Hauptzeitmass. (𝅗𝅥 mässiger.)***
**Molto vivace.**
***Sehr lebhaft.***

ff
sempre stacc.

ment before the group formed by the lovers. Brangæna descends from the turret at the same time and rushes to-
*setzt der Gruppe der Liebenden gegenüber an. Brangäne kommt zugleich von der Zinne herab und stürzt auf Isolde zu.*

ff

wards Isolda. The latter with instinctive shame, leans with averted face upon the flowery bank. Tristan with
*Diese, von unwillkürlicher Scham ergriffen, lehnt sich, mit abgewandtem Gesicht, auf die Blumenbank. Tristan in*

equally instinctive action, streches out his mantle with one arm, so as to conceal Isolda from the eyes of the
*ebenfalls unwillkürlicher Bewegung, streckt mit dem einen Arme den Mantel breit aus, so dass er Isolde vor den*

newcomers. — In this position he remains for some time, fixing his gaze immovably upon the men, who with
*Blicken der Ankommenden verdeckt. — In dieser Stellung verbleibt er längere Zeit, unbeweglich den starren Blick*

various emotions turn their eyes upon him. — Morning dawns. —)
*auf die Männer gerichtet, die in verschiedener Bewegung die Augen auf ihn heften. — Morgendämmerung. —)*

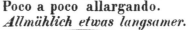

**Poco a poco allargando.**

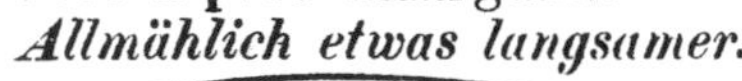

TRISTAN.
TRISTAN.
Con moto moderato.
Mässig bewegt.
MELOT (to Mark).
MELOT (zu Marke).
The drea-ry day its last time comes!
Der ö-de Tag zum letz-ten Mal!
Now say to me, my sov'reign, was my im-peachment just? I staked my head there-on, now is the pledge re-deemed? Be-hold him in the ve-ry act! Honour and fame faith-fully I have saved from shame for thee.
Das sollst du, Herr, mir sa-gen, ob ich ihn recht ver-klagt? Das dir zum Pfand ich gab, ob ich mein Haupt ge-wahrt? Ich zeigt' ihn dir in off'-ner That: Namen und Ehr' hab' ich ge-treu vor Schan-de dir be-wahrt.
p poco cresc.
Lento moderato.
Müssig langsam.
MARK (violently affected, then with trembling voice).
MARKE (nach tiefer Erschütterung, mit bebender Stimme).
Hast thou preserved them? Say'st thou so?
Tha-test du's wirk-lich? Wähnst du das?
molto espressivo dim.
sehr ausdrucksvoll
cresc.

con molto portamento
sehr getragen
See him there, the tru - est of all true hearts;
Sieh' ihn dort, den Treu'sten al - ler Treu - en;
f dim.
p
p
p
look on him, the faith - fullest of friends, too!
blick' auf ihn, den freundlichsten der Freun - de:
His of -
sei - ner
p
p
p
fence so black and base fills my heart with anguish and dis - grace!
Treu - e frei'- ste That traf mein Herz mit feindlichstem Ver - rath!
poco cresc.
più cresc.
ff
Tristan traitor, what hope stayeth that the
Trog mich Tristan, sollt' ich hoffen, was sein
dim.
p
poco cresc.
poco riten.
etwas zurückhaltend
hon - our he be - trayeth should by Melot's rede, rest to me in -
Trü - gen mir ge - troffen, sei durch Melot's Rath redlich mir be -
poco riten.
f
p
più p

Vivace.
Lebhaft.
TRISTAN (with convulsive violence).
TRISTAN (krampfhaft heftig).
accel.
deed? Day - light phan - toms! morn - ing vi - sions, empty and
wahrt? Tags - ge - spen - ster! Mor - gen - träu - me! täuschend und
fp
cresc.
rallent.
MARK (with deep emotion).
MARKE (mit tiefer Ergriffenheit).
vain! a - way! be - gone! This blow,
wüst! Entschwebt! Entweicht! Mir dies?
più f
ff
dim.
p
Lento moderato, come prima.
Wieder mässig langsam.
Molto ritenuto.
Sehr zurückhaltend.
Poco animato, ma in tempo.
Etwas bewegter, doch streng im Zeitmass.
(Bewegter.)
Tris - tan, to me? Where now has truth fled if Tris - tan can be -
Dies, Tri - stan, mir? Wo - hin nun Treu - e, da Tri - stan mich be -
ff
più p
pp
tray? Where now are faith and friendship fair, when from the fount of faith, from Tris -
trog? Wo - hin nun Ehr' und ech - te Art, da al - ler Eh - ren Hort, da Tri -
riten.
- tan they are gone? The buck - ler Tristan once did don, where is that
- stan sie ver - lor? Die Tri - stan sich zum Schild er - kor, wo - hin ist
f
ten.

Largamente.
Breit.
rallent.
(lento)
(langsam)
shield of Vir - tue now when from my friend it flies, and Tris tan's honour
Tu - gend nun ent - floh'n, da mei - nen Freund sie flieht, da Tri - stan mich ver -
f
rallent.
dim.
p
p
Lento moderato, come prima.
Wieder mässig langsam.
(Tristan slowly drops his eyes towards the ground; in his features increasing sorrow is visible as Mark continues.)
(Tristan senkt langsam den Blick zu Boden; in seinen Mienen ist, während Marke fortfährt, zunehmende Trauer zu lesen.)
dies?
rieth?
espressivo e dolce
ausdrucksvoll und weich
p
p
cresc.
f
dim.
Animando.
Belebend.
Why hast thou noble service done, and honour, fame, and potent might a - massed
Wo - zu die Dienste oh - ne Zahl, der Ehren Ruhm, der Grösse Macht, die Mar -
p
p
poco cresc.
Più animando.
Mehr belebend.
— for Mark, thy king? must hon - our, fame, pow'r, and might, must all thy nob - le service
- ken du gewannst; musst' Ehr' und Ruhm, Gröss' und Macht, muss - te die Dienste oh - ne
p
cresc.
done be paid with Mark's dis - honour? Seemed the re -
Zahl dir Mar - ke's Schmach be - zahlen? Dünk - te zu
f
f
dim.
più p

ward too slight and scant, that what thy hand has won him, realms and rich-es, thou art the
we-nig dich sein Dank, dass, was du ihm er-wor-ben, Ruhm und Reich, er zu Erb' und
heir un-to, all? When childless he lost once a
Ei- - - gen dir gab? Da kin-der-los einst schwand sein
p
p
p
wife, he loved thee so that ne'er a-gain did Mark desire to marry.
Weib, so liebt' er dich, dass nie aufs Neu' sich Mar-ke wollt' ver-mählen.
cresc.
mf
dim.
p
Con moto.
Belebt.
When all his subjects, high and low, de-mands and pray'rs on him did press to
Da al-les Volk zu Hof und Land mit Bitt' und Dräu-en in ihn drang, die
p
cresc.
choose himself a consort, a queen to give the kingdom, when thou thy-
Kö-ni-gin dem Lan-de, die Gat-tin sich zu kie-sen; da sel-ber
f
dim.
p

self thy unc-le urged that what the court and coun-try pleaded well—might be con-ceded, op-
du den Ohm beschworst, des Ho-fes Wunsch, des Lan-des Wil-len güt-lich zu er-füllen: in
p
cresc.
mf
p
pos-ing both high and low, op-pos-ing e'en thy-self with kind-ly
Wehr wi-der Hof und Land, in Wehr selbst ge-gen dich, mit List und
cresc.
f
cunning still did he re-fuse, till, Tristan, thou didst threaten, for
Gü-te wei-ger-te er sich, bis, Tristan, du ihm drohtest, für
p
f
p ten.
mf
Animando.
Belebend.
ev-er to leave both court and land if thou receiv-edst not command, a
immer zu mei-den Hof und Land, wür-dest du sel-ber nicht ent-sandt, dem
f
p
cresc.
rallentando
zurückhaltend
Molto più lento.
Viel langsamer.
bride for the king to woo; then so he let thee do.—
Kö-nig die Braut zu frei'n. Da liess er's denn so sein.—
f
p
p

dolcissimo
sehr zart
This wondrous love-ly wife, thy might for me did win, who could be-
Diess wunder-vol-le Weib, das mir dein Muth ge-wann, wer durft' es
dolce
p zart
espress.
dolcissimo
sehr zart
hold her, who ad-dress her, who in pride and bliss-pos-sess her, but would
se-hen, wer es ken-nen, wer mit Stol-ze sein- es nen-nen, oh-ne
p
p
poco cresc.
più cresc.
bless his happy for-tune? She whom I have paid respect to ev-er, whom I
se-lig sich zu prei-sen? Der mein Wil-le nie zu na-hen wag-te, der mein
f
p
owned yet possess'd her nev-er, she, the princess proud and peer-less, lighting
Wunsch ehrfurchtscheu ent-sag-te, die so herrlich hold er-ha-ben mir die
più p
p dolce
poco cresc.
up my life so cheer- -less, 'spite foes, without fear, the fairest of brides
See-le muss-te la- -ben, trotz Feind und Ge-fahr, die fürstli-che Braut
f
f
f

Più animato.
Wieder bewegter.
thou didst bring me here.
brachtest du mir dar.
Now that so gracious a gift was gained my heart less pre-pared was soon-er
Nun, da durch solchen Be-sitz mein Herz du fühl-sa-mer schufst als sonst dem
pained, where it lay o-pen, un-de-fended, thy blow de-scended: hope is
Schmerz, dort wo am weichsten, zart und of-fen, würd'ich ge-troffen, nie zu
end-ed and none can solace or heal me. O why so fiercely, un-
hof-fen, dass je ich könnte ge-sun-den: warum so sehrend, Un-
hap-py man, this stroke dids thou deal me? Pierced by thy dagger's poi-sonous
se-li-ger, dort nun mich ver-wun-den? Dort mit der Waf-fe quä-lendem

point, my heart and soul are rav-aged with ruth; now that my
Gift, das Sinn und Hirn mir sen-gend ver-sehrt, das mir dem
f
p
cresc.
poco accel.
friend has failed in his truth; my trust-ing heart is tor-tured with
Freund die Treu-e ver-wehrt, mein off'-nes Herz er-füllt mit Ver-
poco accel.
f
dim.
p
f
pp
rallent.
doubt; and must I fol-low his steps ab-out, by night list-ning and
dacht, dass ich nun heimlich in dunk-ler Nacht den Freund lau-schend be-
rallent.
poco cresc.
dim.
spy-ing, but to find my own honour dy-ing?
schlei-che, meiner Eh-ren En-de er-rei-che?
pp
molto cresc.
ff
p molto cresc.
Why in hell
Die kein Him-
ff

riten.
a tempo
must I bide with-out hope of a heaven?
-mel er-löst, wa-rum mir die-se Höl-le?
riten. a tempo
ff
ff
dim.
rallent.
molto rallent.
Why en-dure dis-grace, un-
Die kein E-lend sühnt, war-
rallent.
molto rallent.
p
Adagio.
Sehr langsam.
a tempo
mol- sehr
healed by tears or grief?
um mir die-se Schmach?
The
Den
a tempo
Sehr langsam.
molto espressivo
sehr ausdrucksvoll
(dolce)
(weich)
pp
to adagio
langsam
un-explained and hid-den cause of all my woes, who will to us dis-
un-er-forsch-lich tief ge-heim-nis-vol-len Grund, wer macht der Welt ihn
p
più p
pp
Adagio.
Langsam.
TRISTAN (raising his eyes pityingly to Mark).
TRISTAN (mitleidig das Auge zu Marke erhebend).
close?
kund?
O monarch, I may not tell thee,
O Kö-nig, das kann ich dir nicht
p
p
più p
pp

truly; what thou dost ask — remains for aye unanswered.
sagen; und was du frägst, das kannst du nie erfahren.
(He turns towards Isolda who looks up yearningly at him.)
(Er wendet sich zu Isolde, die sehnsüchtig zu ihm aufblickt.)
espress.
mf dim.
più p
rallent.
morendo
Lento moderato. (The ♩ slower than the previous ♪.)
Mässig langsam. (♩ langsamer als zuvor ♪.)
tranquillo
ruhig
TRISTAN.
TRISTAN.
Where Tristan now is going wilt thou, Isolda, follow?
Wohin nun Tristan scheidet, willst du, Isold', ihm folgen?
dim.
più p
pp
poco riten.
The land that Tristan means of sunlight has no
Dem Land, das Tristan meint, der Sonne Licht nicht
poco riten.

a tempo
gleams; it is the dark a - bode of night, from whence I first came forth to
scheint: es ist das dun - kel - nächt' - ge Land, da - raus die Mut - ter mich ent -
a tempo
dolce
light, and she who bore me thence in an - guish gave up her life — nor
sandt, als, den im To - de sie em - pfan - gen, im Tod sie liess an das
più p
long — did languish. She but looked on my face, then
Licht — ge - lan - gen. Was, da sie mich ge - bar, ihr
p
poco riten.
sought this rest - ing place, this land where Night doth reign, where Tristan once hath
Lie - bes - ber - ge war, das Wun - der - reich der Nacht, aus der ich einst er -
poco riten.
p dolce
a tempo
lain: now thither of - fers he thy faithful guide to be; so let I -
wacht: das bie - tet dir Tri - stan, da - hin geht er vor - an; ob sie ihm
a tempo
p dolce
cresc.

sol - da straight de - clare if she will meet him there!
fol - ge treu und hold, das sag' ihm nun I - sold'!
f
dim.
più p
pp
Con moto.
Etwas bewegt.
ISOLDA.
ISOLDE.
When to a foreign land be - fore thou didst in - vite, to
Als für ein fremdes Land der Freund sie ein - stens warb, dem
p
p
ritenuto
zurückhaltend
rall.
a tempo
thee, traitor, rest - ing true, did I - sol - da fol - low. Thy king - dom now art
Un - holden treu und hold musst' I - sol - de fol - gen. Nun führst du in dein
più lento
langsamer
poco riten.
a tempo
p
più
pp
p
più p
pp
show - ing, where sure - ly we are go - ing; why should I shun that land by
Ei - gen, dein Er - be mir zu zei - gen; wie flöh' ich wohl das Land, das
pp

riten. - - - - - a tempo
which the world is spann'd? For Tristan's house and home I - sold will make her
al - le Welt um - spannt? Wo Tristan's Haus und Heim, da kehr' I - sol - de
più p
dolce
rallent.
molto rit.
own: the road where - by we have to go I pray thee quick - ly
ein: auf dem sie fol - ge treu und hold, den Weg nun zeig' I -
cresc.
f
dim.
p
più p
pp
Lento e ritardando.
Langsam und zögernd.
(Tristan bends slowly down to her and imprints a soft kiss on her forehead.)
(Tristan neigt sich langsam über sie und küsst sie sanft auf die Stirn.)
show!
sold'!
dolcissimo
pp sehr zart
(Melot starts furiously forward.)
(Melot fährt wüthend auf.)
morendo
cresc.
Tempo vivo.
Lebhaftes Zeitmass.
MELOT (drawing his sword).
MELOT (das Schwert ziehend).
Thou villain! Ha! A - venge - thee, monarch! Say, wilt suffer such scorn?
Ver - räther! Ha! Zur Ra - che, Kö - nig! Dul - dest du die - se Schmach?
f

TRISTAN (draws his sword and turns quickly round).
TRISTAN (zieht sein Schwert und wendet sich schnell um).
Who's he will set his life a - gainst mine?
Wer wagt sein Le - ben an das mei - ne?
più f
ff
sf
dim.
p
cresc.
(Casting a look at Melot.)
(Er heftet den Blick auf Melot.)
This was my friend, he told me he lov'd me tru - ly; my
Mein Freund war der, er minn - te mich hoch und theu - er; um
poco ritenuto
etwas zurückhaltend
accel.
f
p
a tempo
fame and hon - - - - our he upheld more than
Ehr' und Ruhm mir war er be - sorgt wie
poco riten.
etwas zurückhaltend
fp
cresc.
p poco riten.

accel.
all men. With arrogance he filled my heart, and led those on
Keiner. Zum Uebermuth trieb er mein Herz; die Schar führt' er,
accel.
cresc.
Più vivo.
Noch lebhafter.
Molto vivace.
Sehr lebhaft.
who prompted me fame and pow'r to augment me by
die mich gedrängt, Ehr' und Ruhm mir zu mehren, dem
molto riten.
Poco meno mosso.
Etwas langsamer.
wed-ding thee to our mon-arch. Thy glance, I-
Kö-nig dich zu ver-mäh-len! Dein Blick, I-
molto riten.
dim.
accel.
riten.
sol-da, glamoured him thus, and, jealous, my friend played me false to
sol-de, blendet' auch ihn, aus Ei-fer ver-rieth mich der Freund dem
accel.
cresc.
riten.

Vivace, come prima.
Wieder lebhaft.
King Mark whom I betrayed!—
Kö - nig, den ich verrieth!—
dim.
p
f
cresc.
(He sets on Melot.)
(Er dringt auf Melot ein.)
Guard thee, Melot!
Wehr' dich! Melot!
f
f

(As Melot streches out his sword to him, Tristan lets his guard fall and sinks wounded into the arms of Kurvenal. Isolda throws herself upon his breast. Mark holds back Melot. The Curtain falls quickly.)
*(Als Melot ihm das Schwert entgegen streckt, lässt Tristan das seinige fallen und sinkt verwundet in Kurwenal's Arme. Isolde stürzt sich an seine Brust. Marke hält Melot zurück. Der Vorhang fällt schnell.)*

ff
ff
ff
ff
f
dim.
p
più p
ff

# Third Act. | Dritter Aufzug.

# Scene I. | Erste Scene.

(The garden of a castle. At one side high castellated buildings, on the other a low breastwork broken by a watchtower; at back the castle-gate. The situation is supposed to be on rocky cliffs; trough openings the view extends over a wide sea horizon. The whole scene gives an impression of being deserted by the owner, badly kept, here and there delapidated and overgrown.

In the foreground inside lies Tristan under the shade of a great lime-tree sleeping on a couch, extended as if lifeless. At his head sits Kurvenal, bending over him in grief, and anxiously listening to his breathing. From without comes the sound of a Shepherd's air.)

*(Burggarten. Zur einen Seite hohe Burggebäude, zur andren eine niedrige Mauerbrüstung, von einer Warte unterbrochen; im Hintergrunde das Burgthor. Die Lage ist auf felsiger Höhe anzunehmen; durch Öffnungen blickt man auf einen weiten Meereshorizont. Das Ganze macht den Eindruck der Herrenlosigkeit, übel gepflegt, hie und da schadhaft und bewachsen.*

*Im Vordergrunde, an der inneren Seite, liegt Tristan unter dem Schatten einer grossen Linde, auf einem Ruhebett schlafend, wie leblos ausgestreckt. Zu Häupten ihm sitzt Kurwenal, in Schmerz über ihn hingebeugt, und sorgsam seinem Athem lauschend. Von der Aussenseite hört man einen Hirtenreigen blasen.)*

(The Shepherd shows the upper half of his body over the breastwork and looks in with interest.)
(Der Hirt erscheint mit dem Oberleibe über der Mauerbrüstung und blickt theilnehmend herein.)
a tempo
(Orchestra.)
(Orchester.)
f
pp
p
SHEPHERD.
HIRT.
(Kurvenal turns his head a little towards him.)
(Kurwenal wendet ein wenig das Haupt nach ihm.)
Kur-ve-nal! Ho! Say, Kur-ve-nal! Tell me, friend! Does he still sleep?
Kur-we-nal! He! Sag' Kur-we-nal! Hör' doch, Freund! Wacht er noch nicht?
sfp
KURVENAL. (He shakes his head sadly.)
KURWENAL. (Er schüttelt traurig mit dem Kopf.)
If he a-woke it would be but for ev-er-more to
Erwachte er, wär's doch nur um für im-mer zu ver-
più p
riten.
a tempo
leave us: un-less we
schei-den: erschien zu-
poco riten.
dolce
zart
find the la-dy-leech; a-lone can she give help.
vor die Är-tin nicht, die einz'-ge, die uns hilft.
tenuto
p poco cresc.
p dolce

SHEPHERD.
HIRT.
See-est thou nought? no ship yet on the sea? Quite an-o-ther
Sah'st du noch nichts? kein Schiff noch auf der See? Ei-ne and're
più p
pp
p
dit-ty then would I play, as merry as ev-er I may.
Wei-se hör-test du dann, so lustig als ich sie nur kann.
cresc.
mf
But tell me tru-ly, trusty friend: why languishes our lord?
Nun sag' auch ehr-lich, alter Freund: was hat's mit unserm Herrn?
dim.
p
p
KURVENAL.
KURWENAL.
Do not ask me, for I can nev-er answer. Watch the
Lass die Fra-ge: du kannst's doch nie er-fahren. Eif-rig
p
cresc.
accel.
sea, if sails come in sight a sprightly me-lo-dy play!
späh', und siehst du ein Schiff, so spie-le lu-stig und hell!
accel.
f

(The Shepherd turns round and scans the sea, shading his eyes with his hand.)
(Der Hirt wendet sich und späht, mit der Hand über'm Aug', nach dem Meer aus.)
SHEPHERD.
HIRT.
Blank appears the sea!
Oed' und leer das Meer!
a tempo
molto steso
sehr gedehnt
f
dim.
più p
pp
(He puts the reed pipe to his mouth and withdraws, playing.)
(Er setzt die Schalmei an den Mund und entfernt sich blasend.)
(Cor Anglais on the Stage.)
(Engl. Horn auf dem Theater.)
p
cresc.
sf
pp
accel.
ritard.
dim.
sf
Lento.
Langsam.
molto allarg.
sehr zögernd
poco a poco morendo
allmählich schwindend
a tempo
TRISTAN (motionless, faintly).
TRISTAN (bewegungslos, dumpf).
(He opens his eyes and slightly turns his head.)
(Er schlägt die Augen auf und wendet das Haupt ein wenig.)
The tune so well known; why wake to that? Where am I?
Die al - te Wei - se; was weckt sie mich? Wo bin ich?
KURVENAL.
KURWENAL.
(Kurvenal starts in surprise.)
(Kurwenal fährt erschrocken auf.)
Ha!
Ha!
poco cresc.

Vivace.
Lebhaft.
KURVENAL.
KURWENAL.
Ha! who is speaking? It is his voice!
Ha! Diese Stim-me! Sei-ne Stim-me!
cresc.
Tris-tan! lov'd one! my lŏrd!
Tri-stan! Her-re! Mein Held!
fp
My Tris-tan!
Mein Tri-stan!
cresc.
TRISTAN (with effort).
TRISTAN (mit Anstrengung).
Who calls me?
Wer ruft mich?
KURVENAL.
KURWENAL.
Life! at last! O thanks be to heav-en!
End-lich! End-lich! Le-ben, o Le-ben!
dim.

poco rallent.
etwas zurückhaltend
Sweet - - - - est life un - to my Tris_tan new - ly
Sü - - - - - sses Le - - - - ben meinem Tri_stan neu ge-
rallent.
Poco lento.
Etwas langsam.
TRISTAN (feebly).
TRISTAN (matt).
giv - en! Kur_venal! thou?_ Where was I? Where am I?
ge - ben! Kur_wenal du?_ Wo war ich? Wo bin ich?
più p
più p
pp
L'istesso tempo.
Vorheriges Zeitmass.
KURVENAL.
KURWENAL.
Where art thou? In safe - ty,
Wo du bist? In Frie - den,
(non troppo staccato)
(nicht kurz gestossen)
cresc.
tran_quil and sure! Ka - - re_ol 'tis:
si - cher und frei! Ka - - - re_ol, Herr:
p
cresc.
TRISTAN.
TRISTAN.
KURVENAL.
KURWENAL.
dost thou not know thy fa - thers' halls? This my fathers'? Look but a_
kennst du die Burg der Vä - ter nicht? Mei - ner Väter? Sieh' dich nur
più p
sf
f
p

TRISTAN.
TRISTAN.
Animando.
Belebend.
KURVENAL.
KURWENAL.
round! What a-woke me? The herdsman's dit - ty
um! Was er-klang mir? Des Hir - ten Wei - se
dim.
p
più p
p
hast thou heard, doubt - less; he heedeth thy herds above on the hills
hör - test du wie - der; am Hü-gel ab hü-tet er dei-ne Her -
cresc.
f
p
f
TRISTAN.
TRISTAN.
KURVENAL.
KURWENAL.
there. Have I herds then? Sir, I say it!
de. Mei - ne Her - de? Herr, das mein'ich!
dim.
p
più p
cresc.
Animando.
Belebend.
Thine art court, cas - tle, all! To thee yet
Dein das Haus, Hof und Burg! Das Volk, ge -
fp
cresc.
true, thy trust - y folk, as best they might, have
treu dem trau - ten Herrn, so gut es konnt', hat's
f
fp
cresc.

held thy home in guard, the gift which once thy goodness
Haus und Hof gepflegt, das einst mein Held zu Erb' und
più f
f p
gave to thy serfs and vas-sals here, when go-ing far away in foreign land to
Ei-gen an Leut' und Volk verschenkt, als Al-les er verliess, in frem-de Land' zu
p cresc.
f
TRISTAN.
TRISTAN.
KURVENAL.
KURWENAL.
dwell. What foreign land? Why! in
zieh'n. In welches Land? Hei! Nach
dim.
p
molto cresc.
Poco largamente.
Ein wenig breiter.
Cornwall: where cool and a-ble all that was bril-liant, bra-ve and
Kornwall: kühn und won-nig, was sich da Glan-zes, Glük-kes und
f
no - - - - ble, Tris-tan, my lord, lightly took!
Eh - - - - ren Tri-stan, mein Held, hehr er-trotzt!
poco rallent.
poco rallent.
f
dim.

Poco più lento.
Etwas langsamer.
TRISTAN.
TRISTAN.
Am I in Cornwall?
Bin ich in Kornwall?
KURVENAL.
KURWENAL.
No, no! in Ka-reol!
Nicht doch: in Ka-reol!
steso
gedehnt
TRISTAN.
TRISTAN.
How came I
Wie kam ich
p
f
dim.
più p
pp
Poco più mosso.
Etwas bewegter.
KURVENAL.
KURWENAL.
here? Hey now! How you came? No horse hither you rode; a ves-sel bore you a-
her? Hei nun! Wie du kamst? Zu Ross rittest du nicht; ein Schifflein führ-te dich
cresc.
dim.
cross:
her:
but on my shoulders down to the ship you had to ride;
doch zu dem Schifflein hier auf den Schultern trug ich dich;
cresc.
Poco ritenuto.
Etwas zurückhaltend.
Sempre stringendo.
Immer mehr belebend.
they are broad: they carried you to the shore.
die sind breit: sie trugen dich dort zum Strand.
Now
Nun
you
bist

are at home, at home
du da - heim, da - heim
cresc.
once more; your
zu Land: im
Poco largamente.
Etwas breiter.
own the land, your na - tive land; all lov'd things now are
ech - ten Land, im Hei - mathland; auf eig' - ner Weid' und
f
immer
sempre f
near you; un - changed the sun doth cheer you. The
Won - ne, im Schein der al - ten Son - ne, dar -
Poco ritenuto.
Etwas zurückhaltend.
wounds from which you languish here all shall end their an -
in von Tod und Wun - den du se - lig sollst ge - sun -
f
dim.

Rallentando, molto poco a poco.
Sehr allmählich ein wenig zurückhaltend.
(He clings to Tristan's breast.)
(Er schmiegt sich an Tristan's Brust.)
guish.
den!
dolce
p zart
più p
espressivo
ausdrucksvoll
dim.
Lento moderato.
Mässig langsam.
TRISTAN.
TRISTAN.
Think'st thou thus? I know 'tis not so. but this I cannot tell thee.
Dünkt dich das? Ich weiss es anders, doch kann ich's dir nicht sa-gen.
pp
pp
Where I a-woke ne'er I was; but where I
Wo ich er-wacht weilt' ich nicht; doch wo ich
wandered I can indeed not tell thee. The sun I could not
weil-te, das kann ich dir nicht sa-gen. Die Son-ne sah ich

see, nor paisage fair, nor people: but, what I saw, I can indeed not
nicht, noch sah ich Land und Leute: doch, was ich sah, das kann ich dir nicht
più p
pp
ppp
tell thee. It was the land from which I once came, and wither I re-
sa-gen. Ich war, wo ich von je ge-we-sen, wo-hin auf je ich
pp
turn: the end-less realm of earth-ly night. One thing on-ly there possessed me:
geh': im wei-ten Reich der Wel-tennacht. Nur ein Wissen dort uns ei-gen:
pp
Adagio.
Sehr langsam.
riten.
blank, un-end-ing, all-ob-li-vion! How fad-ed all fore-bodings!
gött-lich ew'-ges Ur-ver-ges-sen! Wie schwand mir sei-ne Ahnung?
ppp
pp
Poco a poco più mosso.
Sehr allmählich belebend.
O,_ wist-ful goadings! Thus I call the thoughts that all t'ward light of day have
Sehn-sücht'-ge Mahnung, nenn' ich dich, die neu dem Licht des Tag's mich zu-ge-
pp
cresc.

press'd me. What on - ly yet doth rest me,
trie - ben? Was ein - zig mir ge - blie - ben,
espress.
poco f
dim. p
cresc.
the love - pains that pos - sessed me, from bliss - ful death's af -
ein heiss - in - brün - stig Lie - ben, aus To - des-Won - ne -
f
dim. p
f
pp
fright now drive me to - ward the light, which de - ceit - ful, bright and
Grau - en jagt's mich, das Licht zu schau - en, das trü - gend hell und
cresc.
p
cresc.
gold - en, round thee, I - sol - da,
gol - den noch dir, I - sol - den,
più f
ff
dim.
p
Animato (ma non allegro).
Belebt (doch nicht schnell).
shines! I - sol - da still in realms of
scheint! I - sol - de noch im Reich der
f
p

sun - - - - - shine! In day - light's radiance still I -
Son - - - - - ne! Im Ta - ges - schim-mer noch I -
sol - - - - da! Ah, what
sol - - - - de! Wel-ches
trem - - - bling! Ah, what yearn - - ing!
Seh - - - nen! Wel ches Ban - - gen!
cresc.
Sempre più animando (l'espressione come il tempo).
Immer mehr belebend (auch im Zeitmass).
To be-hold her how I'm burn - ing!
Sie zu se - - hen, welch' Ver-lan - gen!
cresc.
Heard I - not but now the crash of the door of death be -
Kra - chend hört' ich hin - ter mir schon des To-des Thor sich
p dim.
più p
cresc.

hind me? Once more stands it wide-ly open; con-strained by sun-light
schliessen: weit nun steht es wie-der offen, der Son-ne Strah-len
pp trem.
poco cresc.
fp più cresc.
stream-ing through my daz-zled eyes a-wa-ken, Night must be now for-
sprengt' es auf; mit hell er-schloss'nen Au-gen muss ich der Nacht ent-
più f
p molto cresc.
Con moto.
Bewegt.
sak-en; to pur-sue her, to be-
tau-chen, sie zu su-chen, sie zu
hold her, o'er her bend-ing, to ex-pire as I en-fold her, bliss-ful
se-hen; sie zu fin-den, in der ein-zig zu ver-ge-hen, zu ent-
dim.
rallent.
Poco steso.
Etwas gedehnt.
end-ing! This am I de-nied. Weak and
schwin-den Tri-stan ist ver-gönnt. Weh, nun
rallent.
più p
sf

wan mas - ters me day - light's
wächst, bleich und bang, mir des
p sf
più f
wak - ing mis - er - y. Glares its bright - ness on my
Ta - ges wil - der Drang; grell und täu - schend sein Ge -
accel.
brain, fil - ling me with fan - cies in -
stirn weckt zu Trug und Wahn mir das
cresc.
sane! Ac -
Hirn! Ver -
riten.
curs - ed day, with cru - el glow!
fluch - ter Tag mit dei - nem Schein!
trem.
fp
cresc.

**Molto mosso.**
*Sehr bewegt.*

**accel.**

Must thou ev - - - - - - - - - - - er wake my
*Wachst du e - - - - - - - - - - - wig mei - ner*

**accel.**

*fp* *cresc.* *ff* *ff trem.*

woe? Must ___ thy light ___ be burning ev - - -
*Pein? Brennt ___ sie e - - wig, die - se Leuch - -*

*dim.*

**Poco a poco ritardando.**
***Sehr allmählich langsamer werdend.***
(Poco a poco calando.)
*(Allmählich abnehmend.)*

- er, e'en by night our hearts to sev - - er? Ah! my
*- te, die selbst Nachts von ihr mich scheuch - te? Ach, I -*

*p*

fair - - - - est, sweet - - - - - est, rar - - est!
*sol - - - - de, sü - - - - - sse Hol - - de!*

*dim.*

When wilt thou, when, ah! when, let the torchlight
*Wann end - lich, wann, ach wann lö - schest du die*

*più p*

Sempre più tranquillo. (more and more faintly)
Immer ruhiger. (immer mehr ermattend)
dwin - dle, that so my bliss may kin - dle?
Zün - de, dass sie mein Glück mir kün - de?
p
(He sinks back gently, exhausted.)
(Er sinkt erschöpft leise zurück.)
The light,— how long it glows!
Das Licht,— wann löscht es aus?
dim.
più p
p
dolce
When will the house re - pose?
Wann wird es Ruh' im Haus?
più p
pp
Moderato cominciando e poi stringendo subito.
Mässig beginnend und schnell bewegter.
KURVENAL (who has been deeply distressed, now quickly rouses himself from his dejection).
KURWENAL (nach grosser Erschütterung aus der Niedergeschlagenheit sich aufraffend).
I once de - fied, through faith to
Der einst ich trotzt', aus Treu' zu
p
p
p cresc.
thee, the one for whom now with thee I'm yearn - - ing.
dir, mit dir nach ihr nun muss ich mich seh - - nen.
Trust in my
Glaub' meinem
f

words: thou soon shalt see her face to face; my tongue
Wort: du sollst sie se-hen, hier und heut'; den Trost
p
cresc.
f
that comfort giv - eth, if on the earth still she liv - eth.
kann ich dir ge - ben, ist sie nur selbst noch am Le - ben.
rallent.
dim.
più p
Più lento.
Langsamer.
TRISTAN (very faintly).
TRISTAN (sehr matt).
Yet burns the beacon's spark, yet is the house not
Noch losch das Licht nicht aus, noch ward's nicht Nacht im
pp
dark: I - sol - da liveth and wakes; her voice through darkness breaks.
Haus: I - sol - de lebt und wacht; sie rief mich aus der Nacht.
più p
Stringendo subito.
Schnell belebend.
KURVENAL.
KURWENAL.
Lives she still, then let new hope de -
Lebt sie denn, so lass dir Hoff - nung

light thee! If fool-ish and dull you hold me, this
la-chen! Muss Kur-we-nal dumm dir gel-ten, heut'
f
p
cresc.
day you must not scold me.
sollst du ihn nicht schel - ten.
f
As dead
Wie todt
dim.
p
lay'st thou since the day when that accurs-ed Mel - ot so foully wounded thee.
lagst du seit dem Tag, da Me-lot, der Ver-ruch - te, dir ei-ne Wun-de schlug.
p
cresc.
f
f
Thy wound was hea - vy; how to heal it?
Die bö - se Wun - de, wie sie hei - len?
dim.
p

Thy simple ser - vant then be-thought that she who
Mir thör'-gem Man - ne dünkt es da, wer einst dir
dolce
p
dolce
p
once closed Mo - rold's wound, with ease the hurt could heal thee that
Mo - rold's Wun - de schloss, der heil - te leicht die Pla - gen, von
p cresc.
Me - lot's sword did deal thee. I found the best
Me - lot's Wehr ge-schla - gen. Die be - ste Ärz
espressivo
ausdrucksvoll
f
ff
of leech - es there, to Corn - wall have I sent for
tin bald ich fand; nach Korn - wall hab' ich aus - ge -
cresc.
her: A trust - y serf sails o'er the
sandt: ein treu - er Mann wohl über's
f

accel.
Molto vivace. TRISTAN (transported).
Sehr lebhaft. TRISTAN (ausser sich).
sea, bringing I-sold' to thee. I-sol-da
Meer bringt dir I-sol-den her. I-sol-de
accel.
comes! I-sol-da nears!
kommt! I-sol-de naht!
(He struggles to find words.)
(Er ringt gleichsam nach Sprache.)
più f
O friend-ship!
O Treu-e!
poco rit.
a tempo
High and ho-ly friend-ship!
Heh-re, hol-de Treu-e!
dim.

(He draws Kurvenal towards him and embraces him.)
(Er zieht Kurwenal an sich und umarmt ihn.)
(con molto fuoco)
(sehr feurig)
molto cresc.
f
Da qui il tempo poco più moderato che nel cominciamento.
Von hier an das Zeitmass etwas mässiger als Anfangs.
O Kur - venal, thou trust - - y heart! my
Mein Kur - wenal, du trau - - ter Freund! Du
f
mf
f
tru - est friend I rank thee; how e'er can Tristan thank thee?
Treu - er oh - ne Wan - ken, wie soll dir Tristan dan - ken?
fp
fp
cresc.
Poco largamente.
Etwas breit.
My shel-ter and shield in fight and strife, in weal and woe thou'rt mine for
Mein Schild, mein Schirm in Kampf und Streit, zu Lust und Leid mir stets be-
f
p
f
dim.
life: Those whom I hate thou hat-est
reit: Wen ich ge - hasst, den hass-test
p
cresc.
f

poco riten.
accel.
too; those whom I love thou lov - est
du; wen ich ge - minnt, den minn - test
accel.
dim.
p
più p
poco riten.
cresc.
a tempo
too. When good king Mark I followed of old,
du. Dem gu - ten Mar - ke, dient' ich ihm hold,
a tempo
ff
p
thou wert to him tru - er than gold!
wie warst du ihm treu - er als Gold!
p dolce
cresc.
Ped.
poco riten.
When I was false to my noble friend, to be -
Musst' ich ver - ra - then den ed - len Herrn, wie be -
poco riten.
ff
p
Sempre stringendo.
Noch beschleunigend.
a tempo
tray him too thou didst descend! Thou art selfless,
trogst du ihn da so gern! Dir nicht ei - gen,
a tempo
p
f
cresc.

Molto ritenuto.
Sehr zurückhaltend.
sole - ly mine; thou feel'st for me when I suffer:
ein - zig mein, mit lei-dest du, wenn ich lei-de:
più f
ff espressivo e ben tenuto
ausdrucksvoll und sehr gehalten
Più allargando.
Noch gedehnter.
Meno largo.
Weniger gedehnt.
but what I suf - fer, thou canst not feel
nur was ich lei - de, das kannst du nicht
dim.
p
Vivace (ma non cominciando troppo presto).
Lebhaft (doch nicht zu schnell beginnend).
for me! This ter - ri-ble yearn - ing in my
lei - den! Dies furcht - ba-re Seh - nen, das mich
fp
cresc. poco a poco
fp
heart; this fe - ver-ish burn - ing's cru - el smart;
sehrt; dies schmach - ten-de Bren - nen, das mich zehrt;
sf
sf
did I but show it, couldst thou but know it,
wollt' ich dir's nen - nen, könn - test du's ken - nen:
sf
sf

Poco a poco sempre più stringendo.
Allmählich immer mehr beschleunigend.
no time here wouldst thou tarry; from tow'r to watch thou wouldst
nicht hier würdest du weilen, zur Warte müsstest du
cresc.
hurry, with all devotion viewing the ocean, with
eilen, mit allen Sinnen sehnend von hinnen, nach
eyes impatiently spying there where a ship's sails are flying.
dorten trachten und spähen, wo ihre Segel sich blähen,
Before the wind she drives to find me, on the wings of love she neareth:
wo vor den Winden, mich zu finden, von der Liebe Drang befeuert,
Isolda hither steereth!
Isolde zu mir steuert!
più f
ff

She nears! She nears! so bold - ly and fast!
Es naht! Es naht mit mu thi - ger Hast!
ff
p cresc.
It waves! It waves! the flag from the mast!
Sie weht, sie weht, die Flag - ge am Mast!
ff
p cresc.
Hur - ra! Hur - ra! She reach - es the
Das Schiff! Das Schiff! Dort streicht es am
f
p
f
bar! Dost thou not see?
Riff! Siehst du es nicht?
p molto cresc.
(con impeto)
(heftig)
Kurvenal! Dost thou not see?
Kurwenal! Siehst du es nicht?
più f
ff

**Lento moderato.**
*Mässig langsam.*

(As Kurvenal hesitates to leave Tristan, who gazes at him in mute expectation, the mournful tune of the shepherd is heard, as at the beginning.)
*(Als Kurwenal, um Tristan nicht zu verlassen, zögert, und dieser in schweigender Spannung auf ihn blickt, ertönt, wie zu Anfang, die klagende Weise des Hirten.)*

trem.
(Cor Anglais on the Stage.)
(Engl. Horn auf dem Theater.)
KURVENAL (dejected).
KURWENAL (niedergeschlagen).
Still is no ship in sight!
Noch ist kein Schiff zu sehn!
dim.
(Tristan has listened with waning excitement and now begins with growing melancholy.)
(Tristan hat mit abnehmender Aufregung gelauscht und beginnt nun mit wachsender Schwermuth.)
TRISTAN.
TRISTAN.
Is this the mean - ing then, thou old pa -
Muss ich dich so verstehn, du al - te

the - tic dit - ty, of all thy sigh - ing sound? ___
ern - ste Wei - se, mit dei - ner Kla - ge Klang? ___
più p
On eve - - ning's
Durch A - - bend -
p
cresc.
breeze it sad - ly rang, when, as a child, my fa - - - ther's
we - hen drang sie bang, als einst dem Kind des Va - - ters
dim.
pp
p
più p
death - news chill'd me; through morn -
Tod ver - kün - det; ___ durch Mor -
dolce
zart
sf
dim.
- ing's mist it stole yet sad - der, when the son his mother's fate ___
- gen - grau - en bang und bän - ger, als der Sohn der Mut - ter Los ___
p
sf
p

Molto ritenuto.
Sehr zurückhaltend.
Poco meno ritenuto.
Etwas weniger zurückgehalten.
was taught. When they who gave me breath both felt the hand of
ver - nahm. Da er mich zeugt' und starb, sie sterbend mich ge -
dim.
più p
pp
p
Tempo primo.
Erstes Zeitmass.
death, to them came al - so through their pain the
bar, die al - te Wei - se sehn - sucht - bang zu
cresc.
f
dim.
più p
ancient dit - ty's yearn - ing strain, which asked me then and asks me
ih - nen wohl auch kla - gend drang, die einst mich frug, und jetzt mich
sf
now: What was the fate be - fore me, to which my moth - er
frägt: zu wel - chem Los er - ko - ren, ich da - mals wohl ge -
accel.
bore me? What was the fate? The strain so
bo - ren? Zu welchem Los? Die al - te
(Cor Anglais on the Stage.)
(Engl. Horn auf dem Theater.)

plaintive now re-peats it: For yearn - - ing,
Wei-se sagt mir's wie-der: mich seh - - nen
dim.
p
f
dim.
and dy - ing! No! ah no! It is not
und ster - ben! Nein! ach nein! So heisst sie
p
f
con tenuto
sehr gehalten
so! Yearn - - - ing! Yearn - -
nicht! Seh - - - nen! Seh - -
più f
Poco stringendo.
Etwas beschleunigend.
ing! Ex - pec - tant Im ex - pir - - ing, not dy - ing
nen! Im Ster - ben mich zu seh - - nen, vor Sehn - sucht
sempre
immer f
più f
Più tranquillo come prima.
Wieder ruhiger, wie zuvor.
of de - sir - ing!
nicht zu ster - ben!
ff
f
dim.

(Cor Anglais on the Stage.)
(Engl. Horn auf dem Theater.)
p
trem.
That deathless sound yearn - ing - ly peals, from
Die nie er - stirbt, seh - nend nun ruft um
p
dim.
death's re - pose 'tward my distant love it flows.
Ster - bens Ruh' sie der fer-nen Ärz - tin zu.
espressivo
ausdrucksvoll
morendo
p
p
dim.
Bleed - ing in the boat I lay, a poisoned wound a-nigh my
Ster - bend lag ich stumm im Kahn, der Wunde Gift dem Herzen
p
dim.
heart: soft - - ly stole the strain of
nah: Sehn - - - sucht kla - gend klang die
p molto cresc.
f
dim.
p

riten.
a tempo
sadness as drift - ing help-less I stray'd down — to Ire - land's maid.
Wei-se; den Se - gel bläh - te der Wind hin — zu Ir - lands Kind.
riten.
a tempo
p
più p
p dolce
Poco animando.
Etwas belebend.
She healed my wounds and soothed their
Die Wun - de, die sie hei - lend
più p
pain; then did she o - pen them a - gain; yet dropped her wea - pon
schloss, riss mit dem Schwert sie wieder los; das Schwert dann a - ber
cresc.
f
and re - lent - ed; a poi - son-potion was pre -
liess sie sin - ken; den Gift - trank gab sie mir zu
trem.
dim.
p
p
f
p
f
sent - ed; and when in this I hoped for my heal - ing, there came a
trin - ken: wie ich da hoff - te ganz zu ge - ne - sen, da war der
pp
cresc.
p
f

fi - - - - er - y spell o'er me steal - - ing, that I
seh - - - - rendste Zau - ber er - le - - - - sen: dass nie
should pe - rish nev - - er, but earn fresh an - guish
ich soll - te ster - - ben, mich ew' - ger Qual ver -
ev - - - er!
er - - ben!
The draught! the draught! the ter - ri - ble draught!
Der Trank! der Trank! der furcht - ba - re Trank!
How it fill'd my frame with fren - zy when quaff'd!
Wie vom Herz zum Hirn er wü - thend mir drang!
f
p
f
p
più f
ff
ffp
ff
dim.
p
cresc.

No help can heal, no death bring peace, and give my hun-ger-ing bo-som peace;
Kein Heil nun kann, kein sü-sser Tod je mich be-frei'n von der Sehn-sucht Noth,
no-where, ah nowhere may I rest: ex-pelled from
nir-gends, ach nirgends find'ich Ruh': mich wirft die
Night to Day un-blest, that ev-er up-on my
Nacht dem Ta-ge zu, um e-wig an mei-nen
poco rall.
a tempo
(Poco strascinante.)
(Etwas schleppend.)
sad-ness the sun may glit-ter in gladness. Ah! how this
Lei-den der Son-ne Au-ge zu weiden. O die-ser
poco rall.
a tempo
f
p
fp
cresc.
più f
ff
sf dim.
sf

sun-light's shri - vel-ling stream, is burn - ing my brain with an an - guish su-
Son - ne sen-gen-der Strahl, wie brennt mir das Hirn sei-ne glü - hen-de
molto cresc.
preme! From all this heat that hor-ri-bly
Qual! Für die - ser Hit - ze hei - sses Ver-
sempre
immer
glow - eth, no cool-ing shade a cov - er be-
schmach - ten, ach, kei - nes Schat - tens küh - lend Um-
stow - eth! In this in - tense and tor - tur-ing
nach - ten! Für die - ser Schmer - zen schreck - li-che
grief, what assuag - ing balsam will lend me re-lief? The ter - ri-ble
Pein, welcher Bal - sam soll-te mir Lind' - rung ver-leih'n? Den furcht - ba-ren
p molto cresc.

draught with this an - guish im - bued! Twas I,
Trank, der der Qual mich ver - traut, ich selbst,
ff
p cresc.
Steso.
Gedehnt.
'twas I by whom it was brewed! From fa -
ich selbst, ich hab' ihn ge - braut! Aus Va -
ff
f
ff
dim.
p
- ther's pangs and moth - er's fears, from past
- ters Noth und Mut - ter - Weh', aus Lie -
cresc.
ff
dim.
p
and pre - sent lov - ers' tears, from laughter and sor - row,
- bes - thrä - nen eh' und je, aus Lachen und Wei - nen,
cresc.
ff
p molto cresc.
Poco più stringendo.
Etwas drängender.
smi - ling and sad - ness have I pre -
Won - nen und Wun - den hab' ich des
più f

pared this po - - tion of mad-ness! Thou I have brewed,
Tran-kes Gif - - te ge - fun-den! Den ich ge - braut,
ff
dim.
thou I cre-a - - ted, to sip
der mir ge-flos - - sen, den Won -
p
ff
dim.
whose rap - ture I have been fa - ted,
ne schlür - fend je ich ge - nos - sen,
p
più f
I curse thee, cow-ard-ly
ver - - flucht sei, furcht - ba-rer
ff dim.
Più largo.
Breiter.
draught! Accursed is he who
Trank! Verflucht, wer dich ge-
espressivo
ausdrucksvoll
dim.
p
f

Presto con fuoco.
Schnell und heftig.
(He sinks back senseless.)
(Er sinkt ohnmächtig zurück.)
quaff'd.
braut!
KURVENAL (who has been vainly striving to calm Tristan, cries out in terror).
KURWENAL (der vergebens Tristan zu mässigen suchte, schreit entsetzt auf).
My master!
Mein Herre!
Tris - tan!
Tris - tan!
Fright - ful en-
Schreck - li - cher
chant - ment!
Zau - ber!
O love's de - ceit!
O Min - ne - trug!
cresc.
Ritenuto.
Zurückhaltend.
(molto portato e largamente)
(sehr getragen und gedehnt)
O pas - sion's pow'r! Most sweet dream 'neath the sun! See the work thou hast
O Lie - bes - zwang! Der Welt hol - de - ster Wahn! Wie ist's um dich ge-
p cresc.
done!
than!
Molto ritard.
Sehr zurückhaltend.
Here lies he now,
Hier liegt er nun,
Moderato.
Mässiger.
the no - blest of knights with his
der won - ni - ge Mann, der wie
dim.
dim.

Poco più vivo.
Etwas lebhafter.
Più steso.
Wieder gedehnter.
pas-sion all oth-ers a-bove. Be-hold what re-ward his ar-dour re-
Kei-ner ge-liebt und ge-minnt. Nun seht, was von ihm sie Dan-kes ge-
f
p
cresc.
f
dim.
Molto moderato.
Sehr mässig.
(with sobbing voice)
(mit schluchzender Stimme)
quites, the one sure reward of love! Art thou then
wann, was je Min-nesich ge-winnt! Bist du nun
cresc.
p
f
p
pp
dead? Liv'st thou not? Hast to the curse succumbed?
todt? Lebst du noch? Hat dich der Fluch ent-führt?
pp
Lento moderato.
Mässig langsam.
(He listens for his breath.)
(Er lauscht seinem Athem.)
(dolcissimo)
(sehr zart)
pp
(piano)
(leise)
O rapture! No! He still moves, he lives!
O Wonne! Nein! Er regt sich, er lebt!
rallent.

(dolce)
(zart)
and gently his lips are stirred.
Wie sanft er die Lip-pen rührt!
p
pp
TRISTAN (beginning very faintly).
TRISTAN (sehr leise beginnend).
dolce
The ship!
Das Schiff?
Is't yet in
Siehst du's noch
KURVENAL.
KURWENAL.
sight?
nicht?
The ship? Be sure 'twill come to-day;
Das Schiff? Ge-wiss, es naht noch heut':
it can-not tar-ry lon-ger.
es kann nicht lang' mehr säu-men.
pp
(dolcissimo)
(sehr zart)
(con espressione sempre crescente)
(mit zunehmendem Ausdruck)

TRISTAN.
TRISTAN.
On board I - sol - da, see, she smiles,
Und drauf I - sol - de, wie sie winkt,
dolcissimo
sehr zart
p
p dolce
espress.
ausdrucksvoll
with the cup that re - - - con - ciles.
wie sie hold mir Süh - - - ne trinkt:
p
dim.
p
p
Dost thou see? Dost thou see her now?
Siehst du sie? Siehst du sie noch nicht?
più p
pp
pp
più p
Molto tranquillo, ma non strascinante.
Sehr ruhig und nicht schleppend.
Full of grace and lov - ing mild - ness
Wie sie se - lig, hehr und mil - de
pp
più p
float - ing o'er the o - cean's wildness? By
wan - delt durch des Meer's Ge - fil - de? Auf

bil - - lows of flow - ers light - ly lift - ed, gent - ly
won - - - ni - ger Blu - men lich - ten Wo - - gen kommt sie
più p
t'ward the land she's drift - ed.
sanft ans Land ge - zo - - gen.
p
p molto espress.
sehr ausdrucksvoll
Her look
Sie lä - - -
f
dim.
p
dolce
Poco largamente.
Etwas breit.
brings me ease and sweet re -
- - chelt mir Trost und sü - - sse
cresc.
ff
dim. poco a
pose; her hand one last re - lief bes - tows.
Ruh', sie führt mir letz - te La - bang zu.
poco
più p
p dolce

cresc.
f
dim.
p
Ah, I - sol - - - - da! I -
Ach, I - sol - - - - de! I -
p dolce
cresc.
f
dim.
Sempre più largamente.
Immer breiter.
Largamente.
Breit.
sol - da! How fair art
sol - de! Wie schön bist
p
più p
Più vivo.
Lebhafter.
thou! And Kur - ve-nal,
du! Und Kur - wenal,
p
(staccato, ma ben tenuto)
(staccato, aber gut gehalten)
p
why! what ails thy sight? A-way and watch for her, fool - ish
wie, du säh'st sie nicht? Hinauf zur War - te, du blö - der
poco cresc.

wight! What I see so well and plain - ly, let not thine eye seek
Wicht! Was so hell und licht ich se - - he, dass das dir nicht ent -
p
Sempre poco a poco animando.
Allmählich immer mehr belebend.
vain - ly! Dost thou not hear? A-way, with speed! Haste to the
ge - he! Hörst du mich nicht? Zur War - te schnell! Ei - lig zur
p espressivo
ausdrucksvoll
ben marcato
cresc.
watch - tow'r! Wilt thou not heed? The ship! the ship! I - sol -
War - te! Bist du zur Stell'? Das Schiff? das Schiff? I - sol -
f
p cresc.
- da's ship! Thou must dis - cern it, must
- den's Schiff? Du musst es se - hen! Musst
f
per - ceive it! The ship! dost thou see it?
es se - hen! Das Schiff? Säh'st du's noch nicht?
ff
trem.

(Whilst Kurvenal, still hesitating, opposes Tristan, the shepherd's pipe is heard without.)
(Während Kurwenal noch zögernd mit Tristan ringt, lässt der Hirt von aussen die Schalmei ertönen.)
KURVENAL (springing joyously up).
KURWENAL (springt freudig auf).
O
O
(Cor Anglais on the Stage.)
(Engl. Horn auf dem Theater.)
Molto vivace.
Sehr lebhaft.
rap - ture! Trans - port!
Won - ne! Freu - de!
(Cor Anglais on the Stage.)
(Engl. Horn auf dem Theater.)
(He rushes to the watch-tower and looks out.)
(Er stürzt auf die Warte und späht aus.)
KURVENAL (breathlessly).
KURWENAL (athemlos).
Ha! the ship! From northward it is near - ing.
Ha! das Schiff! Von Nor-den seh' ich's na - hen.
molto cresc.

TRISTAN.
TRISTAN.
So I knew! So I said! Yes, she yet lives, and
Wusst' ich's nicht? Sagt' ich's nicht? dass sie noch lebt, noch
ff
dim.
p cresc.
life to me gives! How could I-sold' from this world be
Le-ben mir webt? Die mir I-sol-de ein-zig ent-
f
f
dim.
free which on-ly holds I-sol-da for me?
hält, wie wär' I-sol-de mir aus der Welt!
(Cor Anglais on the Stage.)
(Engl. Horn auf dem Theater.)
p
f
ff
KURVENAL (shouting).
KURWENAL (jauchzend).
A-hoy! A-hoy! See her bravely tack-ing! How full the
Hei-ha! Heiha! Wie es mu-thig steu-ert! Wie stark der
TRISTAN.
TRISTAN.
can-vas is filled! How she darts, how she flies! The pennon? The pen-non?
Se-gel sich bläht! Wie es jagt, wie es fliegt! Die Flagge? Die Flag-ge?
f (Orchestra.)
(Orchester.)
p
f
p
f sempre stacc.

KURVENAL.
Kurwenal.
A flag is float-ing at mast-head,
Der Freu - de Flag-ge am Wim-pel
f
f
f
fp
cresc. poco a
joy-ous and bright!
lu-stig und hell!
TRISTAN.
Tristan.
A-ha! what joy! Now through the day-light
Ha-hei, der Freu-de! Hell am Ta-ge zu
poco
comes I-sol-da! I-sol-
mir I-sol-de! I-sol-
più f
da! oh come!
de zu mir!
ff
See'st thou her-self?
Siehst du sie selbst?
KURVENAL.
Kurwenal.
The ship is shut
Jetzt schwand das Schiff
meno f
dim.

TRISTAN.
TRISTAN.
from me by rocks. Behind the reef? Is there not
hin-ter dem Fels. Hin-ter dem Riff? Bringt es Ge-
p
Più presto.
Noch schneller.
risk? Those dan-ger-ous breakers
fahr? Dort wü-thet die Brandung,
ff
f
ff
KURV.
KURW.
ships have oft shat-tered! Who steer-eth the helm? The
schei-tern die Schif-fe! Das Steu-er, wer führt's? Der
f
TRISTAN.
TRISTAN.
stead-i-est sea-man Be-trays he me? Is he Me-lot's al-
si-cherste See-mann. Ver-rieth er mich? Wär' er Me-lot's Ge-
ff
ff
ff
ff
KURVENAL.
KURWENAL.
TRISTAN.
TRISTAN.
ly? Trust him like me! A trai-tor thou too!
noss? Trau' ihm wie mir! Ver-rä-ther auch du!
sempre più ff
ff

Ancora più accel.
Noch mehr beschleunigend.
O cai - tiff! Canst thou not see her?
Un - sel' - ger! Siehst du sie wie - der?
ff
KURVENAL.
KURWENAL.
Not yet.
Noch nicht.
TRISTAN.
TRISTAN.
Des-
Ver-
truc - tion.
lo - ren!
ff
Tempo primo.
Früheres Zeitmass.
(Cor Anglais on the Stage.)
(Engl. Horn auf der Bühne.)
ff
3
p
KURVENAL (shouting).
KURWENAL (jauchzend).
3
A-ha! Hal-la-hal-loa!
Heiha! Hei-ha-ha - ha!
They clear! They clear! safe - ly they clear!
Vor-bei! Vor-bei! Glück-lich vor-bei!
(Orchestra.)
(Orchester.)
cresc.
ff
TRISTAN (shouting).
TRISTAN (jauchzend).
Hal-la-hal-loa!
Heiha-ha-ha!
Kur - ve-nal, trust - - - i-est friend!
Kur - - we-nal, treu - - - - e - ster Freund!
ff

All the wealth I own
All' mein Hab' und Gut
poco dim.
to-day I be-queath thee.
ver-erb' ich noch heu-te.
più dim.
p
poco cresc.
KURVENAL.
KURWENAL.
With speed they ap-proach.
Sie na-hen im Flug.
TRISTAN.
TRISTAN.
Now dost thou see her? See'st thou I-sol-da?
Siehst du sie end-lich? Siehst du I-sol-de?
KURVENAL.
KURWENAL.
'Tis she! She waves!
Sie ist's! Sie winkt!
f
p
f
TRISTAN.
TRISTAN.
O wo-man di-vine!
O se-lig-stes Weib!
p
cresc.
f

KURVENAL.
KURWENAL.
The ship is in port!
Im Ha - - fen der Kiel!
più f
più f
I-sol - da! Ha! with but one leap light-ly she
I-sol - de, ha! mit ei-nem Sprung springt sie vom
ff
fp
cresc.
TRISTAN. Sempre accelerando.
TRISTAN. Immer beschleunigend.
springs to land! De-scend from the watch-tow'r, in - do-lent ga-zer! A-
Bord ans Land. Her - ab von der War-te, mü - ssi-ger Gaf-fer! Hin-
f
KURVENAL.
KURWENAL.
way! a-way to the shore! Help her! Help my be-lov'd! In a trice, she shall
ab! Hinab an den Strand! Hilf ihr! Hilf meiner Frau! Sie trag' ich her-
ff
poco riten.
accel.
come; trust to my strong arm! But thou, Tristan, hold thee tran-quil-ly here!
auf: trau' meinen Ar-men! Doch du, Tristan, bleib' mir treu-lich am Bett!
poco riten.
accel.
f
f
dim.
cresc.

## Scene II. | Zweite Scene.

**Molto vivace.**
***Sehr lebhaft.***

(Kurvenal hastens away.—Tristan tosses on his couch in the greatest excitement.)
*(Kurwenal eilt fort.—Tristan, in höchster Aufregung auf dem Lager sich mühend.)*

accel.
turous mad - ness! Can I bear to lie couched here in
di-ges Ra - sen! Auf des La - gers Bann, wie sie er -
accel.
sempre più f
qui - et! A - way! let me fly to where hearts run ri - ot!
tra - gen! Wohl-auf und dar-an, wo die Her - zen schla - gen!
ff
Tris - tan, the brave, ex - ult - ing in strength, has torn him -
Tri - stan, der Held, in ju - beln-der Kraft, hat sich vom
p
cresc.
(He raises himself quite up.)
(Er richtet sich hoch auf.)
self from death at lenght. All bleed - ing and wound - ed Sir
Tod em - por - ge-rafft. Mit blu - ten-der Wun - de be -
f
più f
ffp
Mo - rold I de - feat - ed: all
kämpft' ich einst Mo - rol - den: mit
p
f
f

bleed - - - - - - - - - ing and wound - ed I - sol - da shall
blu - - - - - - - - - ten der Wun - de er - jag' ich mir
più f
f molto cresc. -
(He tears the bandage from his wound.)
(Er reisst sich den Verband der Wunde auf.)
now be greet - ed! Ha-ha, my blood!
heut' I - sol - den! Hei-a, mein Blut!
ff
(He springs from his bed and staggers forward.)
(Er springt vom Lager herab und schwankt vorwärts.)
Mer - ry - ly flows it. She who can help my
lu - stig nun flie - sse! Die mir die Wun - de
ff
accel.
wound and close it, she comes in her pride, she comes to my aid! Be
e - - wig schlie - sse, sie naht wie ein Held, sie naht mir zum Heil! Ver -
accel.
p
cresc. -
space de - fied: let the u - ni - verse fade!
geh' die Welt mei - ner jauch - zen - den Eil'!

(He totters to the centre of the Stage.)
(Er taumelt nach der Mitte der Bühne.)
ISOLDA (without).
ISOLDE (von aussen).
Tris - - tan! Be - lov - - - ed!
Tri - - stan! Ge - lieb - - - ter!
più f
ff trem.
dim.
TRISTAN (in frantic excitement).
TRISTAN (in der furchtbarsten Aufregung).
What! hails me the light? the torch - light, ha!
Wie, hör' ich das Licht? die Leuch - te, ha!
p
The torch is ex - tinct! I come! I come!
Die Leuch - te ver - lischt! Zu ihr! Zu ihr!
f
p
molto cresc.
(Isolda hastens breathlessly in. Tristan, out of his senses, staggers wildly towards her. They meet in the centre of the Stage; she receives him in her arms.)
(Isolde eilt athemlos herein. Tristan, seiner nicht mächtig, stürzt sich ihr schwankend entgegen. In der Mitte der Bühne begegnen sie sich; sie empfängt ihn in ihren Armen.)
ff sempre
Poco a poco allargando.
Sehr allmählich nachlassend im Zeitmass.
ff

ISOLDA. (Tristan sinks slowly to the ground in Isolda's arms.)
ISOLDE. (Tristan sinkt langsam in Isoldens Armen zu Boden.)
Tris - - - tan!
Tri - - - stan!
dim.
Ah!
Ha!
p
molto espressivo
sehr ausdrucksvoll
p
più p
Adagio.
Sehr langsam.
p
TRISTAN (raising his dying eyes to Isolda).
TRISTAN (sterbend zu Isolden aufblickend).
I - sol - da!
I - sol - de!
(He dies.)
(Er stirbt.)
ISOLDA.
ISOLDE.
p
Ha!
Ha!
Animato.
Bewegt.
'Tis I, 'tis
Ich bin's, ich
dolce
più p
pp
p
accel.
Poco ritenuto.
Etwas zurückhaltend.
I, dear - ly be - lov'd! Wake, and once more hark to my voice! I - sol - da
bin's, sü - sse-ster Freund! Auf, noch ein-mal hör' meinen Ruf! I - sol - de
accel.
cresc.
f
ff

Piu ritenuto.
Noch mehr zurückhaltend.
Lento moderato.
Mässig langsam.
calls, I - sol - da comes with Tris - tan — true — to pe - rish!
ruft: I - sol - de kam, mit Tri - stan — treu — zu ster - ben!
ff
dim.
p
Più vivo.
Belebter.
Speak un - to me! But for one mo - ment, on - ly one mo - ment
Bleibst du mir stumm? Nur ei - ne Stun - de, nur ei - ne Stun - de
pp
cresc.
Animato.
Belebt.
Poco steso.
Etwas gedehnt.
op - en thine eyes! Such wea - ry
blei - be mir wach! So ban - ge
molto cresc.
f
molto espress.
sehr ausdrucksvoll
dim.
p
rallent.
days — I waited and longed, that one sing - le hour — with thee I might a -
Ta - ge wach - te sie seh - nend, um ei - ne Stun - de mit dir noch zu
rallent.
p
cresc.
p
Lento moderato.
Mässig langsam.
Animando.
Belebend.
wak - en. Betrayed am I then? Deprived by Tristan of this one so - ly - ta - ry,
wa - chen. Betrügt I - sol - den, be - trügt sie Tristan um die - ses ein - zi - ge
espressivo
ausdrucksvoll
più p
cresc.

Rallentando.
Zurückhaltend.
Molto ritenuto.
Sehr zurückhaltend.
swift_ly fleet_ing, fi_ _ _ _ _ _ _ nal earth_ly joy?
e_wig kur_ze, letz_ _ _ _ _ _ _ te Wel_tenglück?
f dim.
p
più p
Più animato.
Bewegter.
His wound though? Where? Can I not heal it? The rap_ _ _ _ _
Die Wun_de? Wo? Lass sie mich hei_len! Dass won_ _ _ _ _
p
cresc.
f
p dolce
p
_ture of night, oh let us feel it! Not of thy
_nig und hehr die Nacht wir thei_len; nicht an der
p
mf
p
wounds, not of thy wounds must thou ex_pire: to_geth_er, at least, let
Wun_de, an der Wun_de stirb' mir nicht: uns Bei_den ver_eint er_
dolce
p zart

Molto ritenuto.
Sehr zurückhaltend.
fade life's en - fee - - - - - - - - bled fire!
lö - sche das Le - - - - - - - - benslicht!
pp
molto espressivo
sehr ausdrucksvoll
How life-less his look! Still his heart! Stayed is his
Ge-brochen der Blick! Still das Herz! Nicht ei - nes
molto espressivo
sehr ausdrucksvoll
più p
p
Più mosso.
Bewegter.
accel.
breath - ing's gen-tle tide! Must I be wail - ing at his
A - thems flücht'ges Weh'n! Muss sie nun jam - merndvordir
accel.
p molto cresc.
ff
Sempre più mosso.
Immer bewegter.
side, who in rap - ture com-ing to seek him, fear - less sailed o'er the
steh'n, die sich won - nig dir zu ver - mäh - len mu - thig kam über's
meno f
più f
f
Molto animato.
Heftig bewegt.
sea? Too late! Des - per - ate man! cast -
Meer? Zu spät! Trot - zi - ger Mann! Strafst
sempre
immer ff
ff
ff

Sempre stringendo.
Immer heftiger.
ing on me this cru - el-est ban! Comes no re-
du mich so mit här - te-stem Bann? Ganz oh - ne
ff
Poco a poco calando.
Allmählich wieder nachlassend.
lief for my load of grief? Si - lent art keep - ing while I am
Huld mei-ner Lei - dens - schuld? Nicht mei-ne Kla - gen darf ich dir
ff poco dim.
rallent. poco a pcoco
weep - ing? But once more, ah! but once a - gain!
sa - gen? Nur ein - mal, ach! nur ein-mal noch!
rallent. poco a pcoco
ff
dim poco a poco
Sempre ritard.
Immer langsamer.
Tris - tan! Ah! hark! He wakes!
Tri - stan! Ha! horch! Er wacht!
dim.
più p
pp
dolcissimo
sehr zart
Lento.
Langsam.
(She sinks down senseless upon his body.)
(Sie sinkt bewusstlos über der Leiche zusammen.)
Be-lov-ed!
Ge-lieb-ter!
p
pp
pp
pp

# Scene III. | Dritte Scene.

(Kurvenal who re-entered close behind Isolda has remained by the entrance in speechless horror, gazing motionless on Tristan. From below is now heard the dull murmur of voices and clash of waepons. The Shepherd clambers over the wall.)

*(Kurwenal war sogleich hinter Isolde zurückgekommen; sprachlos in furchtbarer Erschütterung hat er dem Auftritte beigewohnt und bewegungslos auf Tristan hingestarrt. Aus der Tiefe hört man jetzt dumpfes Gemurmel und Waffengeklirr. Der Hirt kommt über die Mauer gestiegen.)*

(Kurvenal starts up in haste and looks over the rampart whilst the shepherd stands apart gazing in consternation on Tristan and Isolda.)

*(Kurwenal fährt heftig auf und blickt über die Brüstung, während der Hirt aus der Ferne erschüttert auf Tristan und Isolde sieht.)*

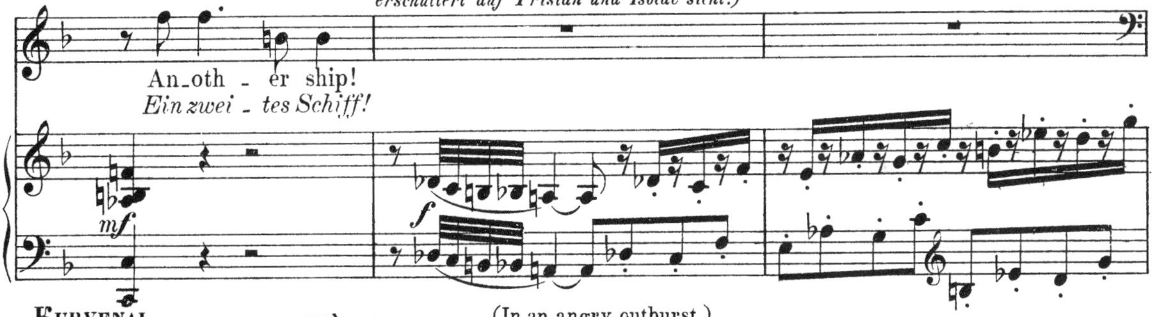

An-oth - er ship!
*Ein zwei - tes Schiff!*

mf f

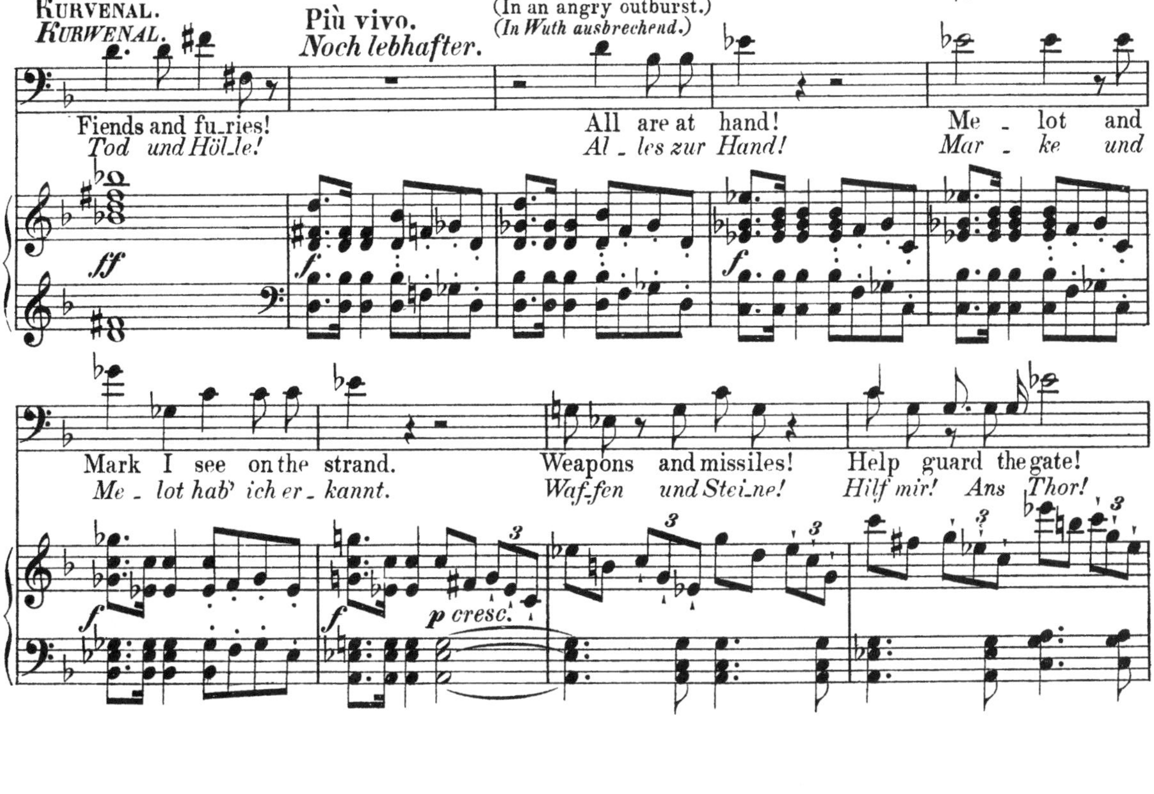

KURVENAL.
*KURWENAL.*

Più vivo.
*Noch lebhafter.*

(In an angry outburst.)
*(In Wuth ausbrechend.)*

Fiends and fu-ries! All are at hand! Me - lot and
*Tod und Höl-le! Al - les zur Hand! Mar - ke und*

ff f f

Mark I see on the strand. Weapons and missiles! Help guard the gate!
*Me - lot hab' ich er - kannt. Waf-fen und Stei-ne! Hilf mir! Ans Thor!*

f f p cresc.

(He hastens with the shepherd to the gate which they try quickly to barricade.)
(Er eilt mit dem Hirten an das Thor, das sie in der Hast zu verrammeln suchen.)
f
ff
ff
THE STEERSMAN (rushing in).
DER STEUERMANN (stürzt herein).
Mark and his men have set on us: de_fence is vain, we're
Mar_ke mir nach mit Mann und Volk: ver_geb'_ne Wehr, be_
p
cresc.
KURVENAL.
KURWENAL.
o_ver_pow_ered. Stand to and help!
wäl_tigt sind wir. Stell' dich, und hilf!
f
f
BRANGÆNA
BRANGÄNE
While lasts my life I'll let no foe_ ent_er here! I_sol_
So lang' ich le_ _ _ _ be lugt mir Kei_nerher_ein! I_sol_
più f
ff
p

(without, calling from below).
(aussen, von unten her).
KURVENAL.
KURWENAL.
(calling down)
(hinabrufend)
- da! Mis - tress! Bran - gæ - na's voice?
- de! Her - rin! Bran - gä - nen's Ruf?
What want you here?
Was suchst du hier?
cresc.
BRANGÆNA.
BRANGÄNE.
Op - en Kur - ve - nal! Where is I - sol - da?
Schliess' nicht Kur - we - nal! Wo ist I - sol - de?
KURVENAL.
KURWENAL.
With foes do you come? Woe to you,
Ver - räth' - rin auch du? Weh' dir, Ver -
cresc.
MELOT (without).
MELOT (ausserhalb).
false one! Stand back, thou fool! Bar not the way!
ruch - te! Zu - rück, du Thor! Stemm' dich nicht dort!
Furioso.
Wild.
KURVENAL (laughing savagely).
KURWENAL (wüthend auflachend).
Hail to the hap - - py day on which I con -
Hei - a - ha - ha! - Dem Tag, an dem ich dich
front thee!
tref - - - - fe!
(Melot with armed men appears under the gateway. Kurvenal falls on him and strikes him down.)
(Melot, mit gewaffneten Männern, erscheint unter dem Thor. Kurwenal stürzt sich auf ihn und streckt ihn zu Boden.)

Die, dam - na-ble wretch!
Stirb', schänd - li-cher Wicht!
MELOT.
MELOT.
Woe's me! Tris - tan!
Weh mir! Tri - stan!
(He dies.)
(Er stirbt.)
BRANGÆNA (still without).
BRANGÄNE (noch ausserhalb).
Kur-ve-nal! mad - man, oh hear! Thou mis-
Kur-we-nal! Wü - thender! Hör; du be -
KURVENAL.
KURWENAL.
ta-kest! Trea-cher-ous maid!
trügst dich! Treu - lo - se Magd!
(to his followers)
(zu den Seinen)
Come! Fol - low! Force them be -
Drauf! Mir nach! Werft sie zu -
(They fight.)
(Sie kämpfen.)
low!
rück!
MARK (without).
MARKE (ausserhalb).
Hold, thou fran - tic man!
Hal - te, Ra - sender!
Lost are thy sen - ses?
Bist du von Sin - nen?
KURVENAL.
KURWENAL.
Here ra -
Hier wü -
cresc.
p
f
mf
ff

va - ges Death!
thet der Tod!
Nought else, oh
Nichts And' - res
King, is here to be holden: if you would earn it, come
Kö - nig, ist hier zu ho - len: Willst du ihn kie - sen, so
(Mark appearing with his followers under the gate.)
(Marke unter dem Thor mit Gefolge erscheinend.)
(He sets upon Mark and his followers.)
(Er dringt auf Marke und dessen Gefolge ein.)
MARK.
MARKE.
on! A - way, rash ma - ni - ac!
komm! Zu - rück! Wahn - - - sin - ni - ger!
(Brangæna has climbed over the wall at side and hastens to the front.)
(Brangäne hat sich seitwärts über die Mauer geschwungen und eilt in den Vordergrund.)
BRANGÆNA.
BRANGÄNE.
I - sol - da! La - dy! Joy and
I - sol - de! Her - rin! Glück und
più f
ffz
fp
cresc.
f
sempre f
più f

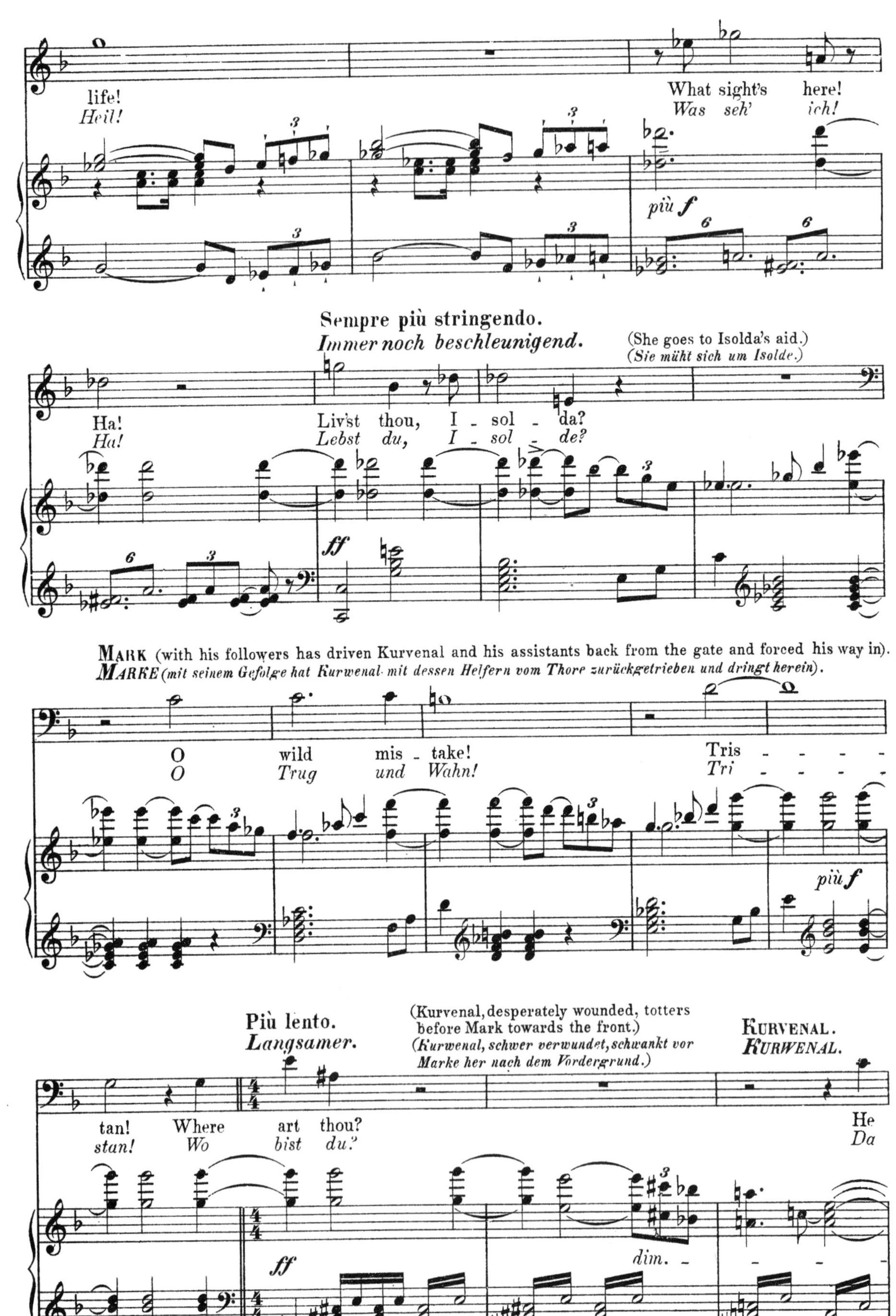
life!
Heil!
What sight's here!
Was seh' ich!
più f
Sempre più stringendo.
Immer noch beschleunigend.
(She goes to Isolda's aid.)
(Sie müht sich um Isolde.)
Ha! Liv'st thou, I - sol - da?
Ha! Lebst du, I - sol - de?
ff
MARK (with his followers has driven Kurvenal and his assistants back from the gate and forced his way in).
MARKE (mit seinem Gefolge hat Kurwenal mit dessen Helfern vom Thore zurückgetrieben und dringt herein).
O wild mis - take! Tris - - - -
O Trug und Wahn! Tri - - - -
più f
Più lento.
Langsamer.
(Kurvenal, desperately wounded, totters before Mark towards the front.)
(Kurwenal, schwer verwundet, schwankt vor Marke her nach dem Vordergrund.)
KURVENAL.
KURWENAL.
tan! Where art thou?
stan! Wo bist du?
He
Da
ff
dim.

Molto ritenuto.
Sehr zurückhaltend.
(He sinks down at Tristan's feet.)
(Er sinkt bei Tristan's Füssen zusammen.)
MARK.
MARKE.
li_eth here, where I lie too.
liegt er, hier, wo ich lie_ge.
Tris_tan! Tris_tan! I_sol_da!
Tri_stan! Tri_stan! I_sol_de!
espressivo
p ausdrucksvoll
dim.
Lento.
Langsam.
KURVENAL (groping for Tristan's hand).
KURWENAL (nach Tristan's Hand fassend).
Woe! Tris_tan! True lord! Chide me not,
Weh! Tri_stan! Trau_ter! Schilt mich nicht,
piu p
espress.
pp
e più p
Ancora più ritenuto.
Noch mehr zurückhaltend.
(He dies.)
(Er stirbt.)
that I try to fol_low thee!
dass der Treu_e auch mit kommt!
p
più p
Moderato.
Mässig.
MARK.
MARKE.
Dead to_geth_er!
Todt denn Al_les!
pp
p espress.
poco cresc.

Più animato.
Bewegter.
All are dead!
Al - - - les todt!
molto espressivo
sehr ausdrucksvoll
My he - ro
Mein Held, mein
p poco a poco cresc.
Tris - tan! Tru - est of friends, must thou a - gain be to thy king a
Tri - stan! Trau - tester Freund, auch heu - te noch musst du den Freund ver -
f
Sempre più animato.
Immer belebter.
trai - tor? Now when he comes an - oth - er proof of love to give thee? A -
ra - then? Heut', wo er kommt dir höch - ste Treu - e zu be - wäh - ren? Er -
p
cresc.
più cresc.
wak - en! A - wak - en! O hear my la - men -
wa - che! Er - wa - che! Er - wa - che mei - nem
molto cresc.
più f
Rallentando.
Zurückhaltend.
(Bending down sobbing over the bodies.)
(Schluchzend über die Leiche sich herabbeugend.)
ta - tion! Thou faith - less,
Jam - mer! Du treu - los
ff
dim.
p

BRANGÆNA (who has revived Isolda in her arms).
BRANGÄNE (die in ihren Armen Isolde wieder zu sich gebracht).
faith - ful friend! She wakes, she lives! I -
treu' - - ster Freund! Sie wacht, sie lebt! I -
pp
p
Animando.
Belebend.
sol-da, hear me! Re-ceive my a - tonement! The love-potion's se-cret to Mark I con -
sol-de! hör' mich, vernimm mei-ne Süh-ne! Des Trankes Ge - heim-nis entdeckt' ich dem
fid-ed: with se-dul-ous haste he put to sea, that he might find thee, no - bly re -
Kö-nig: mit sor-gen-der Eil' stach er in See, dich zu er - rei-chen, dir zu ent -
poco cresc.
piu cresc.
nounce thee and give thee up to thy love.
sa - - - gen, dir zu - zu - füh - - ren den Freund!
f
dim.
Moderato con moto.
Mässig bewegt.
MARK.
MARKE.
O why, I-sol - da, why this to me? When clear-ly dis -
War - um, I-sol - de, war - um mir das? Da hell mir ent -
dolce

closed what be - fore I could fath - om not, what joy was mine to find my friend was
hüllt, was zu - vor ich nicht fas - sen konnt; wie se - lig, dass den Freund ich frei von
poco cresc.
p
Animando.
Belebend.
free from fault! In haste to wed thee to my
Schuld da fand! Dem hol - den Mann dich zu ver -
p
poco cresc.
he - ro, with fly - ing sails I fol - lowed thy track. But
mäh - len, mit vol - len Se - geln flog ich dir nach. Doch
how - e'er can hap - pi - ness o - ver - take the swift course of woe? More
Un - glü - ckes Un - ge - stüm, wie er - reicht es, wer Frie - den bringt? Die
ff
f
p
cresc.
poco accel.
food for Death did I make; more wrong grew in mis -
Ern - te mehrt' ich dem Tod. Der Wahn häuf - te die
poco accel.
più f
ff
ff

Rallentando poco a poco.
Allmählich zurückhaltend.
BRANGÆNA.
BRANGÄNE.
(Isolda unconscious of all around her, turns her eyes with rising inspira-
(Isolde, die nichts um sich her vernommen, heftet das Auge mit wachsender Be-
take! Dost thou not hear? I-sol-da! La-dy! O try to be-lieve the truth!
Noth! Hörst du uns nicht? I-sol-de! Trau-te! Ver-nimmst du die Treu-e nicht?
p
tion on Tristan's body.)
geisterung auf Tristan's Leiche.)
Molto moderato cominciare.
Sehr mässig beginnend.
ISOLDA.
ISOLDE.
pp
Mild and soft-ly he is smil-ing; how his eye-lids
Mild und lei-se wie er lä-chelt, wie das Au-ge
pp
sweet-ly op-en! See, oh comrades! See you not how he beameth
hold er öff-net, seht ihr, Freunde, säh't ihr's nicht? Im-mer lich-ter
p cresc.
ev- - er bright - er, steeped in star-light,
wie er leuch - - - tet, Stern - um - strah-let
p molto cresc.

Poco più animato.
Etwas bewegter.
borne a_bove?
hoch sich hebt?
See you not
Seht ihr's nicht?
f
dim.
p dolce
Ped. * Ped. *
sempre con Pedale
how his heart with li - - on zest
Wie das Herz ihm mu - - thig schwillt,
sempre molto tranquillo
immer sehr ruhig
calm - - - ly hap - - - - - - - - - py,
voll und hehr im
p
beats in his breast?
Bu - sen ihm quillt?
From his
Wie den
p

lips in heav'n - ly
Lip - pen, won - nig
p dolce
p
rest sweet - est breath he
mild sü - sser A - them
p dolce
p
soft - ly sends.
sanft ent - weht.
p
p dolce
p
Hark - en, friends! Hear and feel ye
Freun - de! Seht! Fühlt und seht ihr's
p dolce
p

not?— Is it I a - lone am hear - ing
nicht? Hö - - re ich nur die - - se Wei - se,
cresc
pp
poco cresc.
sempre con Pedale
strains so ten - der and en - dear - - - - - ing? Pas - - -
die so wun - der - voll und lei - - - - - se, Won - - -
8
dim.
più p
pp
- - - - - - - - - - - - sion— swel - - ling, all— things
- - - - - - - - - - - - ne— kla - - gend, Al - - les—
8
dolce
tel - ling, gent - - - - ly - bound - - ing, from— him—
sa - - gend, mild ——— ver - söh - - nend aus— ihm—
più p

sound - ing, in me push-es, up-ward rush-es trum - pet tone that round me
tö - - nend, in mich drin-get, auf sich schwinget, hold er-hal-lend um mich
morendo
pp
cresc.
gush - - - - - - - - - - - - - - - - - - es?
klin - - - - - - - - - - - - - - - - - - get?
tr
molto cresc.
Bright - - er grow - - - ing o'er me
Hel - - - ler schal - - - lend, mich um -
f
p
flow - - - ing, are these bree - - zes' air - - - y
wal - - - lend, sind es Wel - - len sanf - - ter

pil - lows? Are they balm - - y beau - - te_ous
Lüf - te? Sind es Wol - - ken' won - - ni_ger
cresc.
bil - - lows? How they rise and gleam and
Düf - te? Wie sie schwel - - len, mich um -
glis - - - ten! Shall I breathe them? Shall I
rau - - schen, soll ich ath - - men, soll ich
lis - - - ten? Shall I sip them, dive with - in — them,
lau - - - schen? Soll ich schlür - fen, un - ter - tau - chen,
pp

to my pant_ing breath_ing win them? In the
süss in Düf_ten mich ver_hau - chen? In dem
cresc.
bree - zes a - round,_ in the har - mo_ny sound, in the
wo - genden Schwall, in dem tö - nenden Schall, in des
world's dri - - - - - - ving whirl -
Welt - A - - - - - - thems we - - - -
ff
wind be drown'd,_ and sink - - -
hen - dem All_ er_trin - - -
dim.
sempre con Pedale

ing, be drink ing,
ken, ver sin ken,
8
in a kiss, high
un be wusst, höch
8
più p
6
5
(Isolda sinks, as if transfigured, in Brangæna's arms
(Isolde sinkt, wie verklärt, in Brangäne's Armen sanft auf
est bliss!
ste Lust!
pp
3
upon Tristan's body. Great emotion and grief of the bystanders. Mark invokes a benediction on the dead.)
Tristan's Leiche. Grosse Rührung und Entrücktheit unter den Umstehenden. Marke segnet die Leichen.)
trem.
rallentando
morendo
pp
(The Curtain falls during the last pause.)
(Der Vorhang fällt während der letzten Fermate.)